**WOMEN
PRESIDENTS'
ORGANIZATION**

50

**FASTEST
GROWING
WOMEN-
OWNED/LED
COMPANIES**™
GUIDE TO GROWTH

DR. MARSHA FIRESTONE & SUSAN JOHNSON

WOMEN PRESIDENTS' ORGANIZATION

50

FASTEST
GROWING
WOMEN-
OWNED/LED
COMPANIES™
GUIDE TO GROWTH

SPONSORED BY:

Published by Advantage, Charleston, South Carolina.
Member of Advantage Media Group.

ADVANTAGE is a registered trademark and the Advantage colophon is a trademark of Advantage Media Group, Inc.

Printed in the United States of America.

ISBN: 978-1-59932-676-4
LCCN: 2016934832

This publication is designed to provide accurate and authoritative information in regard to the subject matter covered. It is sold with the understanding that the publisher is not engaged in rendering legal, accounting, or other professional services. If legal advice or other expert assistance is required, the services of a competent professional person should be sought.

Advantage Media Group is proud to be a part of the Tree Neutral® program. Tree Neutral offsets the number of trees consumed in the production and printing of this book by taking proactive steps such as planting trees in direct proportion to the number of trees used to print books. To learn more about Tree Neutral, please visit www.treeneutral.com. To learn more about Advantage's commitment to being a responsible steward of the environment, please visit www.advantagefamily.com/green

Advantage Media Group is a publisher of business, self-improvement, and professional development books and online learning. We help entrepreneurs, business leaders, and professionals share their Stories, Passion, and Knowledge to help others Learn & Grow. Do you have a manuscript or book idea that you would like us to consider for publishing? Please visit advantagefamily.com or call 1.866.775.1696.

This book is dedicated to women business owners and leaders who have accelerated the growth of their enterprises and who have, as a result, created more opportunity for economic security for themselves, their employees, and their families.

"The book is truly inspirational and gives visibility to amazing women who have built their businesses through dedication and perseverance. Women need more recognition like this to inspire other women to take the risk, take the chance, and go for it! More visibility for these women and others like them is needed to be role models for young women who are just starting out and may question whether it can be done. And the testimonials and experiences written about are great learning tools to help other women understand how to scale up their businesses and aspire to achieve growth. Congratulations, WPO!"

NANCY PLOEGER
Executive Director, International Women's Entrepreneurial Challenge

"This book is an important testimonial to the tenacity, persever- ance, and capacity that women entrepreneurs possess and is a 'go-to' guide for entrepreneurs that want to scale and grow their businesses. A powerful roadmap to success!"

CARLA HARRIS
Vice Chairman, Wealth Management, Morgan Stanley; Chair, National Women's Business Council

"Don't miss this opportunity to learn from experts on the most important growth topics. These leaders have proven strategies and successful growth stories that have worked for them and *will* work for you!"

PAMELA A PRINCE-EASON, MAS, CPSM
President & CEO, Women's Business Enterprise National Council

TABLE OF CONTENTS

CHAPTER 3

JUNE RESSLER
President and CEO, Cenergy International Services

SONJA N. HINES
President, H&S Resources Corporation

LESLIE A. FIRTELL, ESQ.
CEO, Tower Legal Solutions

CHAPTER 4

PHYLLIS NEWHOUSE
President and CEO, Xtreme Solutions, Inc.

DENISE WILSON
President and CEO, Desert Jet

KARA TROTT
CEO, Quantum Health

CHAPTER 5

SHAZI VISRAM
Founder and CEO, Happy Family

SHARI SPIRO
CEO, Ad Magic Games

CINDY MONROE
Founder and CEO, Thirty-One Gifts

SUSAN SOBBOTT
PRESIDENT, GLOBAL COMMERCIAL PAYMENTS
AMERICAN EXPRESS COMPANY

Leading a company through steady growth is no small feat. It takes vision, passion, perseverance, willingness to take risks, and a lot of hard work. It also helps to have expert advice along the way.

Women are starting businesses at a rate 1.5 times the national average[1]. Women-owned/led middle-market companies generate combined revenues of more than $743 billion and were collectively responsible for more than 6.4 million jobs in 2014.[2] As a middle-market (defined as $10 million to $1 billion in annual revenue) company leader in the US, you are making outsized contributions to the US economy and adding to the success of your employees and customers. Our goal at American Express is to contribute to your continued success and growth, and that is why we are pleased to partner with the Women Presidents' Organization in the creation of this *50 Fastest Growing Women-Owned/ Led Companies™ Guide to Growth*, a tool that will help you think about the future of your company. In it, you will find advice and insights from some of the previous years' 50 Fastest-Growing Women-Owned/Led Companies. These leaders illustrate the broad spectrum of industries in which women excel today. From IT solutions to facility operations management and shipping to custom board games to organic meals and snacks, they have generously shared what has and hasn't worked as they scaled their businesses in five key areas: branding, financing, human resources, innovation, and sales.

You'll hear from women business leaders including:

---

1 | 2015 State of Women-Owned Businesses Report commissioned by American Express OPEN

2 | The Middle Market Power Index: The Growing Economic Clout of Diverse Middle Market Firms from American Express and Dun & Bradstreet

- Nina Vaca, president and chief executive officer of Pinnacle Group, an IT workforce-solutions firm based in Dallas. Nina saw her nineteen-year-old company, which she founded at age twenty-four with $300 of startup capital, more than quadruple revenue in four years from nearly $165 million in 2010 to nearly $666 million in 2014.

- Lacy Starling, who leads logistics provider Legion Logistics, LLC, the Florence, Kentucky-based firm that more than doubled revenue in two years (nearly $12 million in 2012 to more than $25 million in 2014) and added nineteen employees during that span.

Each of these leaders has successfully guided her company to surmount the initial hurdles to growth.

We hope their stories and the tips offered in this guide inspire and direct you as you steer your company through growth and continued success.

For more information about growth strategies and preparing your business for new challenges, please visit: https://business.american-express.com/us/business-trends-and-insights. For more information about American Express Global Corporate Payments, please visit www.americanexpress.com/corporate.

WOMEN PRESIDENTS' ORGANIZATION. Reaching Farther. Together.   WPO 50 Fastest Growing Women-Owned/Led Companies Guide to Growth Sponsored by American Express

2

DR. MARSHA FIRESTONE
PRESIDENT AND FOUNDER
WOMEN PRESIDENTS' ORGANIZATION

We are so very pleased to partner with American Express Global Corporate Payments to help us honor fifteen exceptional women by sharing their inspirational stories.

The growing power of women's businesses and its profound impact on the economy has not received the attention it deserves. So the Women Presidents' Organization decided to do something about it. In 2007, WPO launched the listing of the 50 Fastest-Growing Women-Owned/ Led Companies to focus much-needed attention on the vital role that women-owned/led companies have in boosting the economy and enhancing overall job growth. It was a hit!

Each year, we receive hundreds of applicants vying for the distinction of being named one of the "50 Fastest." The widely anticipated list generates significant media coverage all over the world. While applicants do not have to be WPO members, all eligible companies are ranked according to a sales growth formula that combines percentage and absolute growth. To be qualified for the ranking, businesses are required to be privately held, woman-owned or led, and to have reached annual revenue of at least $500,000.

This book is an acknowledgement of the power of the 50. We called upon fifteen winners in the last few years to share personal stories of tribulations and triumphs related to the five areas that change most when a business scales—branding, financing, human resources, innovation, and sales.

We wanted the inside scoop. What were the bumps they encountered along the way? What did it feel like when they first realized all the hard work and sacrifice was worth it? They also reveal tips—the key ingredients in their "secret sauce" of fast growth.

Women business leaders encounter unique challenges and deserve a supportive resource that provides the knowledge and skills to excel. WPO members take part in professionally facilitated peer-learning groups conducted in a proprietary roundtable format to accelerate the growth of their businesses.

Over the years, we have seen dramatic growth of WPO member businesses. Collectively, our members generate $22 billion. According to the annual Business Outlook Survey we conduct of WPO members:

- 67 percent say their business has grown since joining WPO.
- 77 percent say their participation in a WPO chapter helps them manage their business.
- 74 percent have conducted business with another WPO member.

I always say that being an entrepreneur is the great equalizer. You create a culture you can believe in, have power and influence, and control your time. And you pay yourself more: 75 percent of our members pay themselves six-figure incomes.

As I look toward the twentieth anniversary of the Women Presidents' Organization, I am gratified and so very proud that the organization I started in 1997 now has 127 chapters on six continents, with 1,900 members worldwide.

WPO chapter locations are indicated on the global map below.

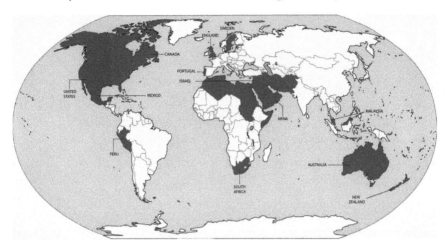

As always, I would like to express my appreciation to our board of directors for their wisdom and commitment. Their energy and enthusiasm enables WPO to continue to provide high-caliber programming for our members and build the prestige of our brand:

Rosa Alfonso-McGoldrick
American Express
Global Corporate Payments

Margery Kraus (Chair)
APCO Worldwide, Inc.

Roz Alford (Secretary)
ASAP Solutions Group LLC

Sharon Lechter
Pay Your Family First

Susan Phillips Bari (Treasurer)
Douglas Elliman Real Estate

Leslie Meingast
TPD

Beth Bronfman
View The Agency

Judi Sheppard Missett
Jazzercise, Inc.

Marsha Firestone, Ph.D. (President)
Women Presidents' Organization

Shirley Moulton (Vice Chair)
The ACADEMi of Life

WOMEN PRESIDENTS' ORGANIZATION. Reaching Farther. Together.
WPO 50 Fastest Growing Women-Owned/Led Companies Guide to Growth Sponsored by American Express

5

Phyllis Newhouse
Xtreme Solutions, Inc.

Racquel Harris
Sam's Club

Tracey Gray-Walker
AXA

Kate Gutman
UPS

Tahir Ayub
PricewaterhouseCoopers, LLP

Joanne Tabellija-Murphy
Walmart

Ana Alleguez
Alleguez Architecture Inc.

Donna Hegdahl
The TransSynergy Group

Juli Betwee
Pivot.Point

Susan Brown
BMO Bank of Montreal

Denise C. Evans
IBM Corporation

Stephanie Sherman
Prudential Financial

Patricia Thomas
Thomas Coaching

Laurie Sinclair
Center for Women in Business

Judith Goldkrand
Wells Fargo

Christine Owens (Retired)
UPS

Jennifer Riley
Chubb

Peggy Turner
Lexus

Allyson Botto
Avis Budget Group

Dino Signore
Edward Lowe Foundation

Beth Marcello
PNC Bank

Annette Hazapis
KeyBank

Robin Pulford
American Airlines

Linda Hamilton (CPA)
Linda A. Hamilton, CPA LLC

Meryl Unger (Counsel)
Katsky Korins, LLP

There is no single path to success. Relationships, innovation, and trust are key ingredients. We hope these stories of accomplishment will encourage and inspire. We hope you will benefit from their wisdom learned along the way and wish you great success in your journey to grow your business so that one day you will be among the 50 Fastest-Growing Women-Owned/Led Companies.

BRANDING

Successful brands create a special relationship with customers, based on a combination of intangible qualities that evoke a strong emotional response. Here, three middle-market entrepreneurs describe their brands and what makes those brands remarkable and memorable.

Lacy Starling
President
Legion Logistics

Nina Vaca
Chairman and CEO
Pinnacle Group

Shelly Sun
CEO
BrightStar Care

LEGION LOGISTICS

LACY STARLING,
PRESIDENT

City, State:
Florence, KY

Year Founded:
2009

Year Won 50 Fastest:
2015

Gross Revenues:
2010:	$	569,679
2012:	$	11,477,196
2014:	$	25,485,107

Business overview:
Legion Logistics is a third-party logistics provider (3PL) connecting customers with products to ship with carriers who can transport them.

To what do you attribute your success?
"I attribute my success to hard work, perseverance, and a positive attitude."

"IT'S ONLY WEIRD
IF YOU MAKE IT
WEIRD."

That's what Lacy Starling says about being in business with her ex-husband.

Describing herself as something of a serial entrepreneur, she was always interested in owning her own business. As an undergraduate pursuing a journalism degree, she started a Web design and marketing

company with fellow students. Initially focused on writing and working in sales, Starling discovered she was the only one in the group who could balance a checkbook. She ended up becoming responsible for all aspects of the company's business management.

Starling's exposure to the logistics industry started early. Her father was a truck driver, and she learned firsthand what a difficult way that was to make a living. Nonetheless, she and her husband opened Legion Logistics six years ago in the basement of their home. They hit their stride in 2010, and by 2011, they grossed $3 million in sales.

"We started the business, and then I found out I was pregnant." Starling's pivotal "make or break moment" came in 2011 when she had a baby girl. Her mother, brother, and husband were all living in the same house, all working for Legion Logistics, and no one was making any money. Lacy gave birth on a Friday, went home from the hospital on Sunday, and was back at work on Monday morning. "The day we brought Catherine home we had $63 in the checking account."

Having a child was the watershed moment that crystallized the urgency to make her business vision work. "Because if it doesn't, then not only is my entire family out on the street, but I have this new child who will suffer along with us." Everyone shifted into high gear and began landing more customers after the baby arrived. In 2012, Legion Logistics brought in $11.7 million, and the company moved out of their home office and into their current location in northern Kentucky (the Cincinnati metropolitan area).

At the end of 2012, Starling and her husband divorced. "We were trying to navigate being divorced and running the business together at the same time." That took a lot of work on both their parts. "It has worked out beautifully for us. Our daughter sees a civilized relationship between us. Everyone sees a civilized relationship. The big joke in the office is it's only weird if you make it weird."

KEEP YOUR EYE
ON THE MONEY

"It's been this rocket-ship growth. In five years we went from zero dollars to $25.4 million." According to Starling, scaling a business requires having a tight grip on the financials. "Having that knowledge and experience in business management, which I brought to the table, is what set us apart. I am a big believer in data and not just instinct. That was really important."

When the company started, Lacy did all the accounting and bookkeeping. Now she has handed off 95 percent of those tasks. "Managing all that data coming in is how you get a true picture of the health of the company."

Her advice: never let someone else control the financial health of your company. "You can have a bookkeeping staff and a great CPA, but as far as understanding and being responsible for the financial health of the company, that falls squarely on my shoulders."

According to a September 2015 Middle Market Power Index report from American Express and Dun & Bradstreet titled "The Growing Economic Clout of Diverse Middle Market Firms," middle-market firms make an outsized contribution to the US

 WOMEN PRESIDENTS'
ORGANIZATION.
Reaching Farther. Together.   WPO 50 Fastest Growing Women-Owned/Led Companies Guide to Growth Sponsored by American Express

13

economy. While representing less than 1 percent of US businesses, they account for 21 percent of business revenues and employ 28 percent of the private-sector workforce nationwide. As of 2014, these companies number more than 136,000, employ more than fifty million workers, and generate nearly $6.2 trillion in revenues.

THERE WILL
BE DIFFICULT
MOMENTS, THEN
THE UNIVERSE
WILL SURPRISE
YOU

"In 2012 we had a huge year. We went from $3.4 million to $11.7 million. Then in 2013, we got our butts kicked." The US government was Starling's largest customer, accounting for 70 percent of her business. In 2013 the government went into sequester, then shut down alto- gether. Legion Logistics's business was slashed. "We still grew that year, from $11.7 million to $15 million. But that was the hardest $15 million we could possibly grind out."

As the adage goes, what doesn't kill you makes you stronger.

Starling learned how to prepare for the lean times—to diversify not only accounts but also her customer base and to sock away more cash. "Having that one awful experience really helped us to think more critically. I always joked at the beginning that we were too dumb to think we would fail. We have added a little bit of humility to the mix."

STRATEGIC
PLANNING IS THE
MOST IMPORTANT
ATTRIBUTE OF
FAST GROWTH

Elevating herself out of the day-to-day was critical in helping Starling to scale her business. She believes that if you don't elevate yourself and if you have to touch everything that comes through the door, you will become the biggest roadblock to getting your company

to scale. "Get yourself out of the day-to-day and into a strategic-planning role to help your company grow so much faster."

PROFESSIONAL
ORGANIZATIONS
FUEL GROWTH

Training, seminars, and peer learning accelerated the speed of Lacy Starling's growth trajectory. "The Women Presidents' Organization is just fantastic. What a wonderfully supportive group of women. You go to your first conference, you meet women who have struggled the same way you have and who are so open to helping each other. They really embrace the idea of growing a community of strong women business owners and presidents. And it's not in a negative way toward men but in a positive 'been there, done that' way, where they have experienced a lot of the same struggles."

Starling recalls one of the speakers at the WPO 2015 annual conference who said that eighteen years ago (at the organization's first conference), she looked out and saw a sea of black pantsuits. "Here in Cincinnati, lately a lot of women have been elevated to C-suite positions. We've created a community to celebrate each other's successes. We are all different. We are able to be who we are and embrace that and not fit into black-pantsuit mode. I look terrible in a black pantsuit."

GIVE YOUR BRAND
A STRONG VOICE

From the beginning, Legion Logistics had a very clear picture of what they wanted the "Legion culture" to look like and what they wanted the brand to be. "We have never had an identity crisis. We have always understood who we are. We work hard, we play hard, and we have a sense of humor. A lot of small startup companies take themselves too seriously in order to sound larger. I think it's a mistake because you sound like a robot."

 WOMEN PRESIDENTS'
ORGANIZATION.
Reaching Farther. Together.   WPO 50 Fastest Growing Women-Owned/Led Companies Guide to Growth Sponsored by American Express

15

A disabled veteran, Starling's ex-husband spent a decade in the military. When he joined the logistics industry, what he found lacking was a consistent customer experience.

The company rebranded in 2014. Creating a uniform experience across all branding touch points is what differentiates Legion Logistics from the competition. Because Starling developed all the content for the website and the marketing materials, the brand had a cohesive, straightforward tone and distinctive look, from email signatures and business cards to the website and telephone system.

"As a $25 million company pursuing business in the midmarket range, it is important that we have a consistent message. When you're tiny, you can get away with being homespun." Since Legion Logistics does not do any advertising, direct mail, or promotions, 80 percent of marketing is through direct customer contact.

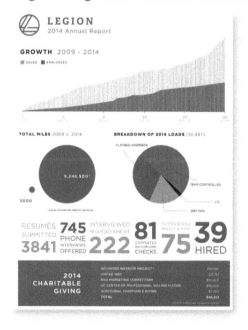

CAPABILITY STATEMENT

Legion Logistics, LLC is a service-disabled veteran-owned third-party logistics (3PL) provider with more than $25 million in sales in 2014.

MC: 694524

DUNS: 831941302

SCAC: LGGS

TAX ID: 27-0890289

NAICS Codes

484110 General Freight Trucking, Local

484121 General Freight Trucking, Long-Distance, Truckload

484122 General Freight Trucking, Long-Distance, Less than Truckload

484220 Specialized Freight (except Used Goods) Trucking, Local

484230 Specialized Freight (except Used Goods) Trucking, Long-Distance

Capabilities

- Experts in third-party logistics solutions for all modes of freight
- Extensive experience with heavy-haul and over-dimensional, dual drivers, temperature controlled, LTL, and expedited shipments
- International ocean and expedited air service
- Focused on creative, nationwide logistics solutions that address needs ranging from single shipments to complex military unit moves and disaster recovery

Differentiators

- VA certified service-disabled veteran-owned small business (SDVOSB)
- Average on-time delivery rate of 97% over the last five years
- EDI (electronic data interchange) capable
- Ranked in top 4% of logistics companies
- Ranked as best broker from 2012 to 2015 by NASTC
- #156 on Inc. 500 in 2014 for exponential growth
- Excellent credit rating with produce Blue Book

Past Performance

- U.S. Department of Defense Surface Deployment and Distribution (SDDC) approved supplier
- Top carrier for Menlo's government services account in volume and service
- Provided assistance to FEMA in delivery of emergency supplies and equipment
- Exceptional service provided with more than 20,000 loads moved since our inception in 2009

LEGION

SERVICE-DISABLED VETERAN OWNED
400 MEIJER DR | SUITE 204 | FLORENCE, KY 41042
p. 859.384.1725 | JOINTHELEGION.COM

GOT A LOT TO SHIP?
BRING IT ON!

Do you have serious shipping needs - like bulldozers that need to get to a construction site in New Jersey or a full load of steel heading to Seattle? The Legion can do that, and much more. We can handle whatever logistics and freight needs you throw our way. We love working with clients to find the best, most affordable and efficient way to get large shipments where they need to be.

We specialize in:

- dry van trailers
- refrigerated trailers
- flatbeds
- removable gooseneck trailers
- oversized and over-dimensional loads with pilot cars

DEDICATED RATES FOR DEDICATED FREIGHT

We offer our customers set rates throughout the year on dedicated lanes. This means our rates won't go up during the produce season capacity crunch, no matter what you ship. All we ask in return is some year-round dedicated freight to keep our carriers moving.

WHAT ELSE DO YOU WANT TO KNOW?

- We are a service-disabled veteran-owned small business
- Our customers enjoy a 98% on-time delivery rate for all loads
- We offer live 24/7 customer service for all of our customers
- We are a Department of Defense approved carrier
- We offer fully customizable freight solutions
- We have over 13,000 qualified carriers ready to ship your products
- We ship over 1,000 loads every month
- We don't give freight back - if we commit to a load we'll cover it, even at a loss to us
- We understand we're moving your future, so we treat your freight as though it were our own.

NOT QUITE CONVINCED? FEEL FREE TO REQUEST CONTACT INFORMATION FOR REFERENCES IN YOUR INDUSTRY!

LEGION

SERVICE-DISABLED VETERAN OWNED
400 MEIJER DR | SUITE 204 | FLORENCE, KY 41042
p. 859.384.1725 | JOINTHELEGION.COM

PROVIDING
UNPARALLELED
CUSTOMER
SERVICE IS
A KEY
DIFFERENTIATOR

The logistics industry must adhere to strict government regulations so all competitors provide the same service. The Legion differentiator: a commitment to provide the absolute best customer service.

"What we do is no different from what other people do. We find a truck, we pay the truck, and you pay us. The transactional piece is the same everywhere you go. The only way it's a unique customer experience is through

our people. What is different is at the other end of the phone."

No matter how large or small her customers are, Starling knows her clients' freight is their livelihood. There is no commerce without distribution. The sole way they make a profit is by selling what they make and getting it into their customers' hands.

"If our customers are watermelon farmers, our mission is to get produce from the field to the store. If they can't get the watermelons to the store, they don't make any money. That's their livelihood."

- Have a solid grasp on your financials. Managing all the data coming in is how you get a true picture of your company's health.

- Keep your eye on the money. Never let someone else control the financial health of your company.

- Anticipate down times before they happen so you are prepared. Diversify accounts and your customer base. Sock away more cash.

- Get yourself out of the day-to-day operations and into a strategic-planning role because it will help your company grow much faster.

- Find a strategic-planning system that forces you to think about growth.

- Know what your end goal is.

- Stay ahead of what's happening, rather than just reacting to it.

- Create a consistent customer experience across all branding touch points.

- Differentiate your business from the competition through flawless customer service.

PINNACLE GROUP

**NINA VACA,
CHAIRMAN
AND CEO**

City, State:
Dallas, TX

Year Founded:
1996

Year Won 50 Fastest:
2015

Gross Revenues:
2010:	$164,567,336
2012:	$235,158,747
2014:	$665,577,015

Business overview:
Pinnacle Group provides contingent labor and software solutions in the workforce-management sector. The company has offices in the US and Canada and provides software solutions globally.

To what do you attribute your success?
"The scalability to meet the needs of a Fortune 500 clientele, coupled with the flexibility and adaptability to design customized solutions for specific business needs."

Nina Vaca has grown Pinnacle Group into one of the most respected and decorated contingent workforce-management firms in the nation. Pinnacle Group has the distinction of being the largest Hispanic-owned and

operated firm in the industry, as well as the fastest-growing woman-owned company in the nation.

Vaca started Pinnacle in 1996 with just $300. It was the beginning of the dot-com era, when technical needs were migrating away from mainframe-computing environments toward more distributed client-server environments. The marketplace was ravenous for information technology talent. Vaca made IT consulting her rapidly expanding niche. Large data centers were being created and Y2K planning was accelerating. It turned out to be a great time to start a technology-centered business.

In 2000, she generated $3.4 million in revenue. However, in the business downturn that followed the NASDAQ crash and the 9/11 terrorist attacks, the rising tide that had sustained her small boutique IT firm quickly dissipated.

Vaca learned a particularly painful but valuable lesson when one of her largest customers offshored the vast majority of its IT work to India, eliminating 75 percent of her business in the process. Though Vaca would eventually double and triple her company on her way to $1 billion, she would never again allow one client to account for such a significant portion of her business portfolio.

Through it all, Vaca never imagined the story of her stratospheric success would wind up in a college textbook. She is included—along with Netflix founder W. Reed Hastings, Jr. and fashion designer Kate Spade—in a chapter of *Understanding Business*, a McGraw-Hill

textbook used to teach entrepreneurship at universities across the country today.

Pinnacle's first make-or-break moment came after nearly a decade of laying the strategic, organizational, and technological foundations to handle a massive expansion of her company. By the first quarter of 2007, Pinnacle was on pace to be a $40 million company. Then everything changed.

Electronic Data Systems (EDS) signed a $180 million contract with Pinnacle, over four times the size of Vaca's company. The complexity of the deal was mind-boggling. It required expanding from five states to a whopping forty-five states. Pinnacle executed contracts with almost 250 subcontractors in the first ninety days. Many of them had never been involved in such a transformative program and questioned Pinnacle's operational and financial ability to handle the change. Pinnacle's balance sheet ballooned. If all of that wasn't stressful enough, Pinnacle had agreed to meet significant performance guarantees and hard-dollar savings commitments.

"I will never forget signing the EDS contract. It was a pivotal, emotional moment for me. An entrepreneur sometimes waits an entire lifetime for a moment like that. I knew our company would never be the same, that the sacrifices made by every one of our people were worth it and would produce something special."

In subsequent years, Pinnacle would sign a series of similar mega-contracts.

"Large customers need to know that their strategic partners can deliver bottom-line results. It's not enough to say that you've done it before. They have to be convinced you can replicate and scale your performance again and again."

Today, Pinnacle Group encompasses several operating companies, including its flagship company, Pinnacle Technical Resources Inc., an award-winning, information-technology, workforce-management provider to the Fortune 500. Pinnacle has grown to become one of the largest providers in its industry, with several thousand consultants across the US and Canada, more than $650 million in annual revenues, and a global footprint that includes the implementation of Provade, its SaaS-based vendor management software (VMS), in more than sixty countries. Collectively, Pinnacle Group manages almost $3.5 billion in annual transaction volume.

According to an April 2015 Middle Market Power Index report from American Express and Dun & Bradstreet titled "Catalyzing US Economic Growth," middle-market firms

are dominant players among privately held enterprises. While the majority of firms with $1 billion or more in revenue are publicly traded, fully 98 percent of middle-market enterprises are privately owned (as are 100 percent of smaller firms). They employ an average of 368 workers, while enterprises with $1 billion or more in revenues employ, on average, 23,226 workers, and those with under $10 million average just four employees per firm.

HARNESS THE POWER OF TECHNOLOGY AND PEOPLE

Vaca urges successful entrepreneurs to focus on customers, culture, and communication. "As you scale and grow, technology becomes a critical enabler of your business. Continuous investment in technology is not a luxury—it's the only way to enable your people to communicate effectively both internally and externally. Without it, you risk losing your people and your culture to more-visionary entrepreneurs who are willing to arm their people with the very best tools available."

She continues, "Always hire top talent and reward them accordingly. Finding the right team members, helping them grow, and positioning them for success has been, and continues to be, a key focus." The need to identify and grow talent is one of her priorities.

"Always, always, always keep the focus on your customer and how to make their business more successful. A CEO needs to look at an entire opportunity to help each client beyond just the immediate needs you may be addressing today. Your customers can never be expected to know all the different ways you can help them. It's your

job to identify those opportunities and put the people and resources in place to deliver results."

"Our growth is a marriage of two things: customers trusting us to serve their strategic business requirements and our ability to execute on those requirements. At a high level it's quite simple, but the day-to-day translation of that into an actionable business strategy and organization is what determines success."

Vaca credits several professional resources along the way with supporting her rapid-growth trajectory. "Years ago I was chosen by Ernst & Young as an Entrepreneur of the Year®, years before the EY Entrepreneurial Winning Women™ program was ever created. After receiving the E&Y award, I became a regional judge, a national judge, and finally a presenter at the national awards gala. The strategic guidance and business relationships attributable to my decade-long involvement with the Entrepreneur of the Year® program continue to benefit me to this day."

In 2015, Vaca was honored as the fastest-growing firm in the Women Presidents' Organization ranking of the 50 Fastest-Growing Women-Owned/Led Companies. "The credibility that distinction brings to our company in the marketplace cannot be measured."

"I am personally grateful to WPO for its leadership in recognizing the contributions of women-owned businesses to our economy. Women have made such amazing progress in the workforce over the past fifty to sixty years, and I am thrilled to be able to inspire the next generation of women business leaders!"

While technology is her passion, Nina Vaca believes nothing takes the place of a face-to-face interaction. She advises business leaders to always take the opportunity to jump on a plane and visit a customer. "Never give up the opportunity to speak to your customers directly. Your customers want to hear from you. They want to know that you are personally engaged and that they are important to you. This becomes even more important as you grow."

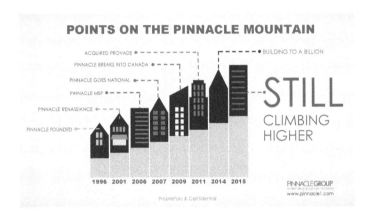

POINTS ON THE PINNACLE MOUNTAIN

Pinnacle Group, which in 2015 rebranded itself from the original Pinnacle Technical Resources, is today a workplace powerhouse with a suite of capabilities that cultivate, procure, and deliver human capital.

The longevity of the Pinnacle management team reflects the long-term impact of vision and values that focus on keeping people happy, well compensated, and empowered to be the best they possibly can be. "We started out with a vision to provide customers with the premier talent they needed to propel their business forward. As the marketplace evolved, so too did Pinnacle. We have embraced cutting-edge business intelligence and state-of-the-art technology, all the while maintaining a people-first culture."

Vaca describes Pinnacle as entrepreneurial, performance driven, imaginative, and innovative. Pinnacle maintains a sophisticated industry perspective driven by business intelligence. Above all, every member of Pinnacle's management team is passionate about community leadership and philanthropy.

Today, Pinnacle operates in a $4 trillion industry through four lines of business, including:

- technology/contingent labor
- managed services provider (MSP)
- payrolling and independent-contractor compliance
- vendor-management software (Provade VMS)

The breadth of Pinnacle's service offerings, combined with its status as one of the very few scalable, diversity-owned providers, positions the firm uniquely within the industry. The company is frequently sought out as both a direct service provider to Fortune 500 clientele and as an attractive strategic partner for larger, global competitors.

BUILT ON A STRATEGY OF "LANDING AND EXPANDING"

"*Land and expand* is industry jargon for cultivating long-term relationships as a trusted advisor to clients. Our goal is not to have hundreds of client relationships. Rather, we aspire to serve a few dozen clients comprehensively, leveraging our full suite of capabilities. In this manner, our customers truly become our business partners, and we are able to have highly strategic, impactful discussions with them about the direction of the industry and their opportunities to remain ahead of key business trends."

"When we engage with our customers, it is very important to us to schedule quarterly strategic reviews both to measure our performance and to be aspirational." Vaca uses these reviews to provide her customers a perspective on industry trends, to address best practices and strategic options, and over time, to measure each quarter's performance trajectory against history.

A CULTURE
BUILT ON
ENTREPRENEURISM

Vaca describes Pinnacle as an entrepreneurial and performance-based culture. "You don't have to be the founder to be an entrepreneur! We have built a culture of entrepreneurship!" She concedes that not everyone aspires to have both the freedom and the responsibility that comes with being a true entrepreneur. "But for the right people, it energizes them in a way that nothing else can. I'm looking for leaders every day. If you think that's you, then welcome to Pinnacle!"

In terms of community involvement, Pinnacle is highly engaged in national and regional organizations that exist to provide procurement opportunities, such as: Women's Business Enterprise National Council (WBENC), National Minority Supplier Development Council (NMSDC), and United States Hispanic Chamber of Commerce (USHCC). She is a frequent speaker for these organizations on topics surrounding entrepreneurship, women's advocacy, diversity, and high growth.

"Pinnacle stands on the shoulders of many organizations that mentored and recognized us long before we became an 'overnight sensation.' It is one of the proudest aspects of my career that I am now able to give back to these groups and inspire future business and community leaders."

"Of course I've made mistakes—probably thousands of them," Vaca admits. "But the key to making mistakes as an entrepreneur is twofold. First, recognize your mistakes early and minimize the dollar exposure. Second, try to make fewer mistakes than your competition, and correct them immediately. Making mistakes used to bother me, but now I embrace it. In fact, if we're not making mistakes all the time, we're not pushing hard enough. It's easy to say but hard to do. If you can truly embrace it, you've crossed one of the critical thresholds toward becoming a leader."

**TIPS FROM
NINA VACA**

- Fail fast: recognize your mistakes early and minimize financial exposure.

- Anticipate customer needs.

- Have personal relationships with your clients—technology can't do that for you.

- Find the right team members, mentor them, and position them for success.

- Use technology as an enabler to grow and scale your business.

- Diversify your revenue base—never allow one customer to represent the majority of your company's business.

- Leverage awards given by professional memberships and regional organizations to build brand visibility.

BRIGHTSTAR CARE

SHELLY SUN,
CEO

City, State:
Gurnee, IL

Year Founded:
2002

Year Won 50 Fastest:
2014

Gross Revenues:
2009: $ 51,732,716
2011: $156,812,048
2013: $249,062,623

Business overview:
BrightStar Care is a premium healthcare-staffing company providing the full continuum of care, from private home care for people of all ages to supplemental staffing for medical facilities, including hospitals, independent/assisted living facilities, and doctors' offices.

To what do you attribute your success:
"The single strategy accounting for our success is my team's unwavering commitment to bringing the vision of making it more possible for families in need of high-quality home care into everything we do on a day-to-day basis. My senior leadership team, our corporate staff, our franchisees, and their office staff and caregivers all work exceptionally hard to develop programs to deliver compassionate, professional care. That model of working

hard, coupled with a commitment to a higher standard of quality, attracts those types of personalities for our corporate team, franchisees, nurses, and caregivers."

IT ALL STARTED WITH GRANDMA PAT

Shelly Sun's fiancée's grandmother was very ill when the Illinois-based couple became engaged in late 2001. They needed to find homecare services for Grandma Pat, services that offered a little bit of everything—from help with activities of daily life (like dressing and bathing) to administering pain medication. But Grandma Pat lived in Florida.

Trained as a CPA, Sun was very detail oriented. But she was not prepared for the complexity of the challenge she was facing: coordinating and overseeing long-distance care giving.

Sun did extensive research, interviewing local discharge planners, nurses, and healthcare professionals, but she could not find one private-pay provider that offered consolidated services. Forced to cobble together multiple providers, she had to monitor logistics and quality control one at a time.

Her emotion-fraught journey—punctuated by confusion, frustration, fear, and isolation—inspired a business idea. Sun saw a marketplace need to provide the same caliber of quality care that adult children would provide their aging loved ones if they lived nearby.

The experience overseeing Grandma Pat's care inspired a commitment to help other families facing the same challenge of providing in-home care for loved ones who chose to "age in place."

Grandma Pat passed away on March 22, 2002, the day before Shelly and her fiancé got married. In memory of what they had searched for and could not find as consumers, they created BrightStar on October 1, 2002.

FRANCHISING
PROVIDES A
FAST-GROWTH
ENGINE

Trust is the premise upon which BrightStar Care is grounded. "I didn't realize at the time what we were on to and what it took to take care of all the Grandma Pats. It has exploded from there."

Sun started her first location in Lake County, Illinois, in 2002 and was very successful. Other sites followed in McHenry County and then a Chicago-based venue in 2003–2004. Her mother-in-law made an investment in two franchise-brand hotels and asked Shelly to invest with her. The notion of providing a consistent customer experience through franchising was born.

Sun had heard about the ATHENA *PowerLink®* program, which guides women business owners in defining and achieving tangible goals by providing free access to business advisors to help them achieve growth and profitability. At the end of 2004, Sun obtained her own board of advisors who helped her evaluate and launch a franchising model. After filing her first agreement with the FTC in summer of 2005, the first franchised Bright-Star location opened in March 2006.

Gaining traction in the beginning was not easy. Sun pitched franchise brokers to put her company in their inventory of business opportunities available for invest-ment. However, unless she could first sign ten franchi-sees, the brokers were not interested. FranNet (which

represents potential franchisees throughout Central Florida, Orlando, and the Greater Tampa Bay Area) put BrightStar in its probationary inventory. Sun's husband tapped his college roommate, a KPMG managing partner in Chicago, for help. "He expected to screen me out. But he thought so highly of our thought process and branding and where we were heading, he not only recommended moving forward, he and his brother even talked about becoming a franchisee."

The positive word of mouth about how well BrightStar franchisees were doing, along with recommendations from brokers, proved to be the tipping point. While Sun said getting those first ten franchisees to take a chance and believe in her business model was harder than going from ten to one hundred, she added, "Once we had early adopters who said how successful they were and how meaningful the business was, it grew like wildfire."

Two years into franchising, the business crossed into midmarket range. The company was on track to do $350 million in 2015.

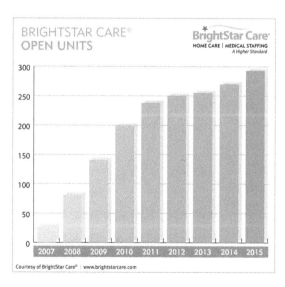

Courtesy of BrightStar Care® | www.brightstarcare.com

Owing to her background as a CPA and the discipline she learned from focusing on checks and balances and consistent processes, leveraging and investing in technology was one of the most important reasons Sun's company was able to scale. "I am the inventor of the patent application of the technology we designed. In 2004, I wrote the design requirements for the technology platform we use and had it coded. We had a consistent technology application before we launched nationally."

Putting everyone on the same Web-based system, enabling remote access, gave franchisees the ability to spot-check the quality and documentation of all operations and to deliver a consistent consumer and employee experience. There was useful data to help franchisees understand how certain behaviors resulted in good outcomes, matching the top and bottom lines to financial results. That information has proved invaluable in growing the business to scale so quickly.

"Starting in 2004, we invested heavily in technology. In 2011 and 2012, we also invested in business intelligence to enable franchisees to have real-time performance metrics available weekly and to see how their performance compared with other franchisees in the system." Using the same platform, they were able to aggregate information and self-correct in real time to optimize business performance.

According to a September 2015 Middle Market Power Index report from American Express and Dun & Bradstreet titled "The Growing Economic Clout of Diverse Middle Market Firms," middle-market firms are

job creators, with 15 percent employing five hundred or more workers, 48 percent between one hundred and 499 workers, and 37 percent fewer than one hundred workers. Among women-owned middle-market firms, 44 percent employ fewer than one hundred workers, 48 percent employ between one hundred and 499, and just 7 percent employ five hundred or more workers. Among minority-owned middle-market firms, 43 percent employ fewer than one hundred workers, 49 percent between one hundred and 499, and 9 percent employ five hundred or more workers.

"OVER HIRE"
DURING TIMES OF
RAPID GROWTH

One of the lessons Sun learned was that during times of heavy growth, you have to anticipate growth and "over hire," choosing talent that is even more experienced than what the job description calls for, in order to own a function and take it forward. This might mean spending 30–40 percent more on salaries than initially anticipated. "Once I figured out that at our growth pace I needed to start hiring to what the role needed to be two years from now, I started to get a lot faster traction. As a CPA, I am cost-conscious, so it took me a while to accept this lesson."

Hiring over the capabilities of talent helped her turn over more and more of the day-to-day business functions so she could focus on strategy. With the right talent in place, she was able to turn over important responsibilities to others and hold people accountable.

Sun is passionate about what she does: serving parents, grandparents, and their adult children. "What allowed us to succeed was having a passion, not just for building a business but for having a purpose and making a difference. We look at franchisees who are not just good business people but who are getting into the business for the right reasons. They need to match our passion and core values first. That's the reason we have been so successful and have grown so quickly."

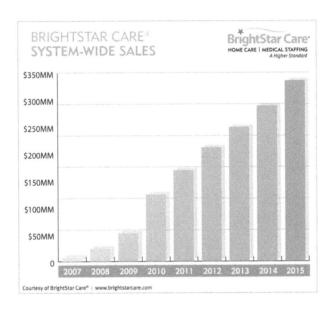

BRIGHTSTAR CARE
SYSTEM-WIDE SALES

BrightStar Care·
HOME CARE | MEDICAL STAFFING
A Higher Standard

Courtesy of BrightStar Care® | www.brightstarcare.com

Sun's customers are largely the "sandwich generation," adults caring for their aging parents while supporting their own children. These are adult children, mainly women forty-five to sixty with aging parents, with $75K annual household income, who are college educated and who live more than seventy-five miles away from their parents. Usually there is some kind of trigger event that signals a parent needs additional care, like forgetting to turn off the stove or wandering away from home and not remembering how to get back.

"We deliver person-centered care according to the highest professional standards. Accreditation, nurse oversight, and highly screened personnel make me confident that we deliver the highest level of care."

In terms of Sun's competition, at the local level there are typically one hundred to two hundred companies providing home care, half paid through Medicare. Sun does not participate in Medicare. "By not taking Medicare, we can spend time focused on quality of care, not on paperwork."

What Sun believes makes her brand remarkable is having extremely high standards:

- commitment to the highest clinical standards
- supervision throughout every client's care journey
- screening/training/supervision of every care giver

Each franchisee has a localized BrightStar Care website, access to branded email templates, Facebook, and Google Plus. There are national and local public relations resources in place. The marketing strategy is focused on making the brand top-of-mind through every step in the care journey.

FOCUS ON CORE VALUES

Shelly Sun believes strong performers, who are also innovative, are more willing to make mistakes and learn from them and to accept accountability and move on. These franchisees have a high sense of integrity and a commitment to doing things the right way, for the right reasons. They do not take short cuts. "If it costs more to do absolutely the right thing, we will absolutely spend more."

Sun has five core values:

- Be open/positive.
- Serve with passion.
- Do the right thing.
- Do what you say.
- Make it great.

Sun believes you can't have a bad day in front of your employees. In order to achieve fast growth, it is important to imbue your professional life with a source of support and great advice. Sun sees it as essential to personal and professional health. "I tried to seek out established resources in an industry sector or category and learn from others. If we are not continuously learning, we are not doing our absolute best."

She joined The Women Presidents' Organization in 2004 and was in a local chapter for four years. She ascended to its Platinum Group (annual gross revenue over $10 million annually and average revenue $44 million) from 2008 to 2014. Having a child with special needs required reducing her travel schedule. Because of this, she left the Platinum Group, as it involves committing to three off-site retreats per year, and plans to soon return to a WPO chapter.

**TIPS FROM
SHELLY SUN**

- Invest in business intelligence to obtain performance metrics available in real time.
- Reinvest in talent and technology as you grow and build your brand.
- Hire people who may be overqualified when you are experiencing heavy growth, so you have the right person in place two years from now.

- Secure access to credit early, before you need it. Banks might be less willing to approve an additional line of credit if you wait until the last minute.

- Start with the end in mind: think big.

- Protect your intellectual property early. Lock in URLs and trademarks when you first start out. While it might be expensive at the time, it's easier sooner than later.

FINANCING

—

Businesses that experience rapid growth face unique financing challenges. In this chapter, three entrepreneurs reflect on how they financed their enterprises and what they learned along the way. Sharing advice with other middle-market companies looking to scale their businesses are:

Mary Kariotis
President and CEO
Merrimak Capital Company

Dr. Rebecca Thomley
President and CEO
Orion Associates/Morning Star Financial Services

Pamela O'Rourke
President and CEO
ICON Information Consultants, LP

MERRIMAK
EQUIPMENT LEASING & ASSET RECOVERY
Copyright 2015 Merrimak Capital Company

MERRIMAK CAPITAL COMPANY

MARY KARIOTIS,
PRESIDENT AND
CEO

City, State:
Novato, CA

Year Founded:
1991

Year Won 50 Fastest:
2015

Gross Revenues:
2010: $ 32,705,382
2012: $ 44,046,764
2014: $108,540,428

Business overview:
Merrimak is a full-service equipment-management and asset-recovery company providing financial solutions that encompass the entire equipment life cycle. Merrimak maximizes resale values and provides sustainable recycling services, delivering solutions to drive tangible cost savings.

To what do you attribute your success:
"Possessing high integrity and enthusiasm while being innovative, transparent, and strategic are the descriptive qualities I possess that I attribute to my success. While finding fulfillment in my own achievements, I covet my employees and customers and am equally empowered by creating success for those whom I work with personally and for the customers we serve."

WOMEN PRESIDENTS'
ORGANIZATION.
Reaching Farther. Together.

As a young UC Berkeley graduate, Mary Kariotis took a job selling telecommunications equipment. When her clients began to lease the equipment from her, a successful thirty-year career began; it would take her to the top of Merrimak, where her leadership has been instrumental to the company's growth.

Merrimak Capital Company started as an asset-recovery company, focusing on the refurbishment, resale, and recycling of IT equipment. Merrimak's global-market focus has expanded to encompass the leasing and fleet management for material handling and is now considered an industry pioneer leader by the clients it serves.

The company manages the entire equipment life cycle for leased or customer-owned assets, driving tangible cost savings through maximizing resale values and providing sustainable recycling services. Merrimak's equipment-management capabilities and material-handling fleet- management services not only focus on competitive financial solutions but also contain maintenance costs and maximize equipment efficacies with statistical data reporting.

As a full-service lessor, Merrimak provides flexible financing solutions; operating, capital, tax, and terminal rental adjustment clause (TRAC) leases, in addition to short-term rental options. Asset tracking and recovery services are available as standalone offerings that generate revenue. As the actual reseller of the off-lease equipment, Merrimak can minimize or eliminate end-of-term chargebacks.

Having been in business since 1991, Kariotis took a leap of faith in 2008. "Our business had evolved to where our lease originations were predominately generated through independent contractors. Though successful, this model did not allow for the growth I envisioned or long-term sustainability."

It takes time to grow a business to scale. According to an April 2015 Middle Market Power Index report from American Express and Dun & Bradstreet titled "Catalyzing US Economic Growth," on average, commercially active small firms have been in business for twelve years, middle market firms for forty-two years, and firms with $1 billion or more in revenue have been in business an average of fifty-two years. Among middle-market firms in particular, 37 percent have been in business for fewer than twenty-five years (and hence are likely to be first-generation firms), 33 percent have been in business between twenty-five and forty-nine years, and 30 percent have been in business for fifty years or more (and thus are on their second or even third generation of owners).

Realizing that her company did not have long-term viability the way it was organized, she completely restructured it and took control by building and leading internal sales with a unified team, eliminating the way she had been generating revenue through independent contractors. By doing so, she lost accounts and walked away from significant guaranteed revenue.

Having reinvented her company, Kariotis went to market with a completely different and ultimately successful strategy that tripled her lease origination revenues. Merrimak now manages some three hundred thousand assets, and since 2009 has added more than fifty of the Fortune 500 and largest private corporations as clients.

In theory at least, the leasing business is a pre-established, monotonous industry. Companies never really know their lessor, fleet-management company, or asset-recovery supplier until the actual transaction is complete.

Sadly, the way most customers learn about leasing is through a bad experience. A customer who signs up for a thirty-six-month lease and does not thoroughly understand the contract implications might be surprised to discover the length of the lease is actually thirty-seven months, due to interim rent collected prior to the lease commencement. Even worse, a client who does not closely scrutinize accounts payable might not realize that the monthly fee was still being paid on equipment that had already been removed or sold, as some lessors will continue to bill regardless.

Kariotis is committed to making a transformational change in an industry that is unregulated, despite the fact that it loans capital. She knows every customer has different levels of knowledge about leasing and that the responsibility for overseeing the function is usually just one aspect of someone's overall job responsibility.

"Customers often don't understand the consequences of the terms and conditions of equipment leasing, even

when they may be a sophisticated Fortune 100. Terms that appear to be benign can in fact be very costly. We want to help our customers drive cost savings and be part of the solution, not gain from their naivety or lack of experience."

The Merrimak approach is based on full disclosure and on making sure its customers are fully aware of all the financial terms of any lease the company originates. The company provides extensive customer education, explaining leasing terms and conditions. "The more educated a customer is about leasing, the more successful Merrimak will always be."

We Are Grateful for Our Customers!!

Serving the Fortune 500 and the Largest U.S. Corporations

UNIQUE SELLING PROPOSITION

Merrimak is one of the few leasing companies that provide in-house refurbishment and remarketing services for off-lease equipment. This results in cost savings for Merrimak customers. Outside equipment brokers, whom other lessors typically utilize to purchase off-lease equipment, pay 20 percent or less below liquidation value, forcing the incumbent lessors to charge excessively for equipment repairs to recapture the residual investment.

"We like to know and understand the assets we lease, to know the entire sales cycle of laptops, servers, forklifts, medical equipment, etc. By controlling the entire life cycle, we understand the product we lease, enabling us to provide better pricing and service than our competition."

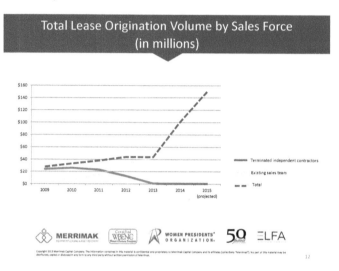

MAKING THE DECISION TO LEASE RATHER THAN BUY

While many clients usually have the cash on hand to purchase equipment, they typically don't want to deal with having to remarket or dispose of retiring equipment. Leasing offers many advantages, such as preservation of capital and hedging against technological obsolescence.

"Our goal is to offer a solution that provides the lowest cost of use to our clients and manages the equipment life cycle, which helps make the decision to lease an easy one. Even with FASB 13 (Financial Accounting Standards Board) going away in 2019, the need to lease will always exist because it increases cash on hand, improves balance sheets, increases efficiencies, provides a competitive edge, and takes customers out of the business of remarketing used equipment."

Recognizing that having accurate, up-to-date information helps in monitoring and controlling expenses, Merrimak developed proprietary software, iTrack, to help clients manage their leased assets and provide comprehensive fleet management for material-handling equipment. Customers also have access to Merrimak's Web-based asset recovery portal, iCycle, where they can schedule online equipment pick-ups in real time, avoiding additional rents that most lessors charge by deliberately making this process difficult and therefore extending the lease.

While focusing on business development is a critical function, Kariotis believes that having timely financial information is the second most important component of fast growth. Constantly monitoring the growth and return on her portfolio, she needs financial reports for her banks and accurate cash management to guide her decision making and to take her company to the next level.

Kariotis tracks:

- portfolio by credit and by equipment type
- total lease originations and asset book value by year
- total lease origination in volume by sales force
- GAAP revenue, income, and EBIDA (earnings before interest, taxes, and amortization) by year
- lease NBV (net book value) by lease types, lease originations by type (capital, operating, or direct finance), and by equipment type
- equity line usage
- residual realization versus booked residual (20 percent return is assumed at lease origination; actual realization tracked at lease end)

- recourse equity by lender (when borrowing the equity) and nonrecourse debt by lenders (payment stream)

- syndication pools under exclusive Merrimak management

- asset-recovery margin and margins realized through equipment recycling and remarketing

USING CREDIT/ EQUITY TO MANAGE BUSINESS

Kariotis recommends weighing the benefits of leveraging cash or credit and types of risk assumption in order to acquire equity funding. It is a matter of striking a delicate balance between how much risk to assume as a function of a greater or lesser return on investment.

"That's what our business is all about: how I can get the lowest equity cost, minimize overhead, and maximize margins. I ask myself whether I would rather take a risk in equipment or share the risk with someone else and have them invest as an equity partner."

Boosting the company's tax basis essentially allows for a tax-free government loan. "Depreciation of assets for a leasing company allows for an increase in the tax basis by temporarily deferring the tax obligation. It is critical not to spend those dollars but instead to increase retained earnings, as some day that money will be due."

Merrimak encourages entrepreneurs to look at the time value of money and how to manage it, while at the same time making sure not to create exposure that results in being placed in a vulnerable position. "The banks don't look at your basis. As long as you have the ability to pay it back down the road, it's a way to leverage cash."

The relationship with local bankers has been somewhat of a challenge. "The local bank for Merrimak's working

capital line has been a struggle. Banks only want to create credit facilities for profitable companies. That makes it challenging for companies that are starting out and building their balance sheets. That's tough. Fortunately, we're in the leasing business, and we have four to five key banks, with two being lead banks, that have been instrumental in supporting and allowing for Merrimak's growth and providing cash flow as needed."

One of her lead banks helped her leverage personal assets to increase additional equity and control the growth of her company.

Also, as a member of the Women Presidents' Organization, Kariotis takes advantage of benefits afforded by corporate sponsors. "I love the Avis Preferred Renter Program available through WPO and am always thrilled to receive the reliable complimentary upgrades."

LOOKING TO THE FUTURE

Kariotis focuses purely on organic growth to achieve her progression and meet targets, a process she likens to guerilla warfare. She is working to develop a plan where employees are vested in the company. However, that is a tricky endeavor, as a vesting program affects her net worth and retained earnings, directly affecting her ability to leverage available low-digit capital to invest in leases. If she decides to sell her company, she wants to offer her employees the upside with some form of a stock-incentive plan.

Thinking about the future, Mary has thought about the possibility of going public. "When Merrimak's EBIDA[1] reaches a certain level, then I am either going to sell or go public."

[1] *Earnings before interest, taxes, depreciation and amortization

- Be innovative and find solutions that improve strategies and drive tangible savings.

- Do not be afraid of change. If you go down the wrong path and have to make a change, do it quickly and do not throw good money after bad.

- Keep your eye on the goals for your business. Don't let logistics distract and sidetrack you. Your primary focus should be on business development.

- Make sure you always have a "Plan B" so you can liquidate or have access to capital, if needed.

- Be a pioneer and find ways to be on the cutting edge in your industry.

- Monitor and keep a tight rein on company spending. Focus on reducing waste.

- Protect your valued employees, but don't be afraid to let go of the ones that don't fit your company model.

- Offer supreme and innovative customer service, but have the courage to walk away from customers who are only looking to gain share for their own benefit.

- Know the labor laws in each state and be in compliance, regardless of how silly the rules may seem to you.

- Don't spend more than you make or can pay back if necessary at any time.

- Consider the cost of using credit. Look at ways to leverage cash.

- Do not pay excessive interest costs. Find ways outside of traditional lending to borrow competitive money.

MORNING STAR
FINANCIAL SERVICES

DR. REBECCA
THOMLEY,
PRESIDENT
AND CEO

City, State:
Golden Valley, MN

Year Founded:
2006

Year Won 50 Fastest:
2015

Gross Revenues:
2010: $ 1,491,222
2012: $ 4,732,590
2014: $ 44,199,555

Business overview:
Morning Star Financial Services is a financial-management firm in the human-services industry providing the highest quality payroll and administrative services to individuals with disabilities, the elderly, and their families. Morning Star provides services in Colorado, Ohio, Oklahoma, Tennessee, and Utah. The company has also worked in Arkansas, Oklahoma, New Jersey, Michigan, Illinois, the Philippines, and Nepal.

To what do you attribute your success:
"We believe that our business success is the result of a combination of creativity, a willingness to take risks, perseverance, and surrounding ourselves with talented people."

As a clinical psychologist who started out seeing patients full time in private practice, Dr. Rebecca Thomley took a nontraditional path into business. Thomley was providing therapy services at an organization in the Twin Cities. When both her parents became ill, she continued to see patients and took an administrative job. Ultimately, she went back to school for a business degree, so she could gain knowledge in running a company.

"The first thing I did was to put together a board of advisors, external people who could look over my work and company operations. I've had a strong team of advisors forever and actively seek and recruit outside opinions or critiques. When you have a background as a clinician, you are used to having every part of your work analyzed in order to grow from that."

Orion Associates manages the administrative and personnel functions of the companies it founded (both for profit and not for profit), which provide a range of specialized social and vocational services for the developmentally disabled, elderly, chronically mentally ill, and their families. Customized for each organization, these services include financial, human resources, and training functions and are delivered with professionalism and compassion by a team with blended expertise in management and psychology.

As Orion grew, it gained insight into the growth potential for broadening its services. In 2003, Orion ISO was spun off to manage the growing portfolio of consumer-directed businesses and is one of Minnesota's largest fiscal agents. Orion Associates, which provides a full range of management services, has been

awarded the highest level of accreditation, assuring its quality programs and services are measurable and accountable.

Thomley has led the organization's efforts to broaden its social-service mission and to promote greater community outreach and volunteerism. A lifelong volunteer, Thomley committed the organization to disaster relief, and in 2005 created the nonprofit Headquarters Relief Organization. That organization has since provided leadership to nearly 1,500 community volunteers. Projects have ranged from cleanup and rebuilding to mental health support delivered in New Orleans; greater Louisiana; southeastern Minnesota; Cedar Rapids, Iowa; Fargo and Minot, North Dakota; and most recently, Minneapolis and Haiti. More than 95 percent of management employees participate regularly in volunteer activities.

INEXPERIENCE DOES NOT MEAN INABILITY

Thomley believes that through hard work and determination anything is possible. Recently, her organization spearheaded the formation of an Internet café in Haiti.

"It was really a struggle because of all the things you need to do in a country with no infrastructure. I am not particularly computer savvy. It would never have occurred to us that if any idea was great we could not do it. You can figure out just about anything. That's a pervasive attitude here. That kind of creative edge is a core part of the business. We want people to think outside the box and take a risk. You'll never get into trouble for taking a risk here and trying to create positive change."

Partnerships have been extremely important in Orion's swift growth. "We have consciously gone out of our way to build partnerships with all kinds of both related and nonrelated organizations. So if we get into trouble with different things, we have lots of resources and lots of good friends."

Several organizations have proved to be particularly helpful to Thomley along her entrepreneurial journey. She joined the EY Entrepreneurial Winning Women program after her son, who started his own business when he was nineteen, was named a regional EY winner. When the program selected her in 2011, she realized what a difficult transition it was for a psychotherapist to go into business. Thomley says, "I did not identify myself as a business woman. I still identify as a psychologist. I did not communicate in the same language. I did not think the same. I felt my feet got knocked out from under me."

Joining the Women Presidents' Organization and getting her organization WBENC certified further expanded her boundaries with resources that had never been a part of her business life. "What I found amazing was how supportive women are of each other in business. Pretty soon I started to do business with people I met. We looked for WBENC vendors. Now some of my best resources are the women I met through these programs."

Both WPO and EY opened the door to networks that offer great support, as she continued with rapid growth in all related companies.

It was a pivotal time. "I feel like I received much more than I have given back in those programs and those friendships. I watched my son grow up with mentors who were excited about working with him. That kind of a system had not existed for me. I thought it's okay; I am older, tougher, and wiser from all these years and will stay my course. But there is nothing more valuable than support from someone else that is going through the same experience. And I didn't have that."

STRENGTHS CAN ALSO BE WEAKNESSES

Looking back on her fast-growth trajectory, Thomley credits not being afraid to take risks as one of the key components of her success. She also believes persistence, what she calls "doggedness," is a key attribute. "It's the old saying that your strengths are also your weaknesses. I never think about giving up. But that's also my weakness. Sometimes I don't know when to quit."

USING FINANCIAL INFORMATION TO GUIDE FAST GROWTH

Like many women entrepreneurs, Thomley self-funded when she started the company, initially relying on funds from another company she owned when she was a clinician in individual practice.

"My base equity put me in a position to put proposals together and leverage a line of credit with the bank for working capital. I also invested in real estate, did some property acquisition, and used resources for expanding." Thomley built sufficient base equity to establish a financial-statement history, which put her in a position to grow and use debt leverage.

Thomley generated the financial resources to fuel her growth through retained earnings that helped generate

more leverage capabilities. By expanding in existing markets and adding geographical reach, she now views herself as a national, multiservice provider.

However, some of the growth her company experienced happened so quickly she was not in a position to plan for it. "If you can have a well-thought-out approach, you could have a more proactive strategy."

Morning Star Financial Services Historical Revenue

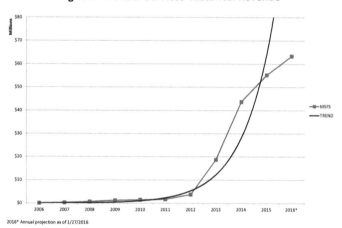

2016* Annual projection as of 1/27/2016

Orion Associates and Related Entities Combined Revenue

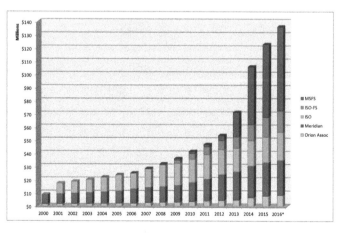

"We leveraged debt financing with our bank with equity that was privately held by the founders in a disciplined and controlled manner of debt to equity ratio. It's important that we have as much financial autonomy as possible to grow our business. If you are overly laden in debt, you lose autonomy. You have to be careful to put tight financial restrictions and governance in place. But we also need a bank that moves at our speed."

In the beginning she relied on hands-on, traditional financial statements. As her organization grew, it needed more customized, specialized financial-reporting systems for supervisors, managers, and clients, to gauge how certain departments were doing.

Credit and charge cards have been part of the entire financial picture and are important for employees. "Credit and charge cards allow quick execution delivery of items bogged down by purchase orders or requisition system." She restricts usage to those with good judgment who are trustworthy. Debts must be turned over each month and paid off.

HAVE A GOOD RELATIONSHIP WITH YOUR BANKER

Thomley believes one of the ways to have a good banking relationship is to always be proactive with extra information before being asked. "When important changes happen, we update budgets and provide new forecasts. We also provide key financial-ratio reports when significant changes have happened, or are about to occur."

If a major change occurs, she gives her bankers advance notice at least forty to ninety days beforehand. "We don't like surprises in our business and don't want our bankers to be surprised, either. We view our bank as a nonequity partner in our business. The more transparent, the better the terms and conditions we have on credit and mortgages."

SUCCESS BASED ON SUPERIOR CUSTOMER SERVICE

Superior service comes from employees who are competent, loyal, and passionate about what they do. Since employees are her most important asset, Thomley strives to make Orion a place where all employees can grow, both personally and professionally. She looks for inventive ways to measure performance and invest in an individual's future—including incentives, supplemental rewards, and financial bonuses—emphasizing training and mandatory professional enhancement training, as well as tuition reimbursement.

"We are a social-services provider. Our success is based on providing superior service in the marketplace. That comes from employees who are competent and loyal and passionate about the service they provide. Employees are our most important assets."

LOOKING TO THE FUTURE

As a social-services provider, a strong social conscience permeates the organization. While she has the option of working with investment capital to provide the equity necessary to fund future growth, Thomley does not find the concept of having business partners particularly appealing. She feels the notion of having business partners who place a higher premium on short-term financial gains may not be the best approach.

"Our reputation, both in the market and in the dedication of our loyal staff, has given us a strong foundation

to grow nationwide. Maximizing short-term profits does not bode well for our growth model."

If an IPO underwriter assured Thomley she would not have to change her business culture and values, she would be open to having a sudden burst of equity to grow the company, although she is not sure it would help her to recruit and retain a new level of management. "Our current team is exceptional. We carefully recruit and develop the next generation of management, without compromising longer-term core values and vision."

- Have a strong advisory group that offers skills you don't have. Always have a legal advisor on board.

- Hire a close team of people whom you trust. Give them the independence and the power to make decisions. Be sure to let them know they are valued.

- Do not be afraid to take risks: growth often comes from taking a gamble.

- Use credit wisely in a controlled ratio balance with equity. If credit is too large relative to equity, your business will be under the spell of lenders.

- Strive to build equity so you can maintain better control of your own destiny.

- Look for creative ways to measure and reward performance of employees.

- Be proactive with your banker by providing extra information before being asked. Provide new forecasts and key financial ratio reports quickly when significant changes have occurred or are about to occur.

- Let credit work for you, and do not allow unpaid debt balances to linger.

ICON INFORMATION CONSULTANTS, LP

PAMELA O'ROURKE, PRESIDENT AND CEO

City, State:
Houston, TX

Year Founded:
1998

Year Won 50 Fastest:
2015

Gross Revenues:

2010:	$125,597,464
2012:	$169,163,280
2014:	$215,058,768

Business overview:
ICON Information Consultants, LP specializes in identifying and recruiting highly qualified professionals in all areas of information technology, accounting, finance, human resources, and procurement, along with a specialized project-management division (iSolutions LTD). The company's primary mission is to deliver high-quality, value-added human capital solutions to Fortune 100 and 500 clients to achieve the most cost-effective business goals.

To what do you attribute your success:
"The secret to success is quite clear: it's all about relationships. It takes years to get and maintain a client, and entrepreneurs cannot afford to give up. Some of my best business relationships have taken years to establish."

WOMEN PRESIDENTS' ORGANIZATION.
Reaching Farther. Together.

When people first meet Pamela O'Rourke, they sometimes comment that she's very quiet. Her response: "It's early."

Early in her career when O'Rourke was working in information technology in corporate America, she marched to the beat of her own drum. When accused of spoiling her clients with extraordinary customer service, she replied that she thought that was what she was supposed to do. After all, she could outperform everyone else. However, her manager talked to her multiple times because she was making her coworkers nervous due to the tremendous amount of energy she devoted to the job. O'Rourke decided it was time to channel that energy and go out on her own.

FAILURE WAS NOT AN OPTION

Since the bank said, "People are not a tangible asset," O'Rourke could not get a loan when she started out. So she wrote a business plan and solicited two groups of friends to invest in the start-up.

Between her own investment and the money that she raised, she opened the business with $250K in capital. Then she gave herself six months to make it work. "My goal was to be the best human-capital solutions IT firm in the USA." Failure was not an option.

Choosing to work only with Fortune 100 and 500 corporations because of their significant investment in state-of-the art technology (and knowing she would get paid), she crossed over into the midmarket range her first year. "I thought I was only going to do $70K my first year. Then I did $2.5 million. The next year was $7.7 million. The third year was $11.7 million, then $14 million

and $16 million. In 2015, revenue exceeded $250 million."

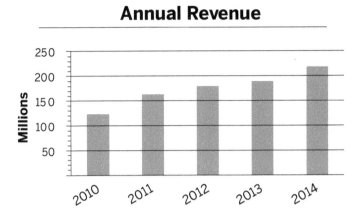

Annual Revenue

ICON Information Consultants pays three thousand consultants throughout the US and Canada on a weekly basis. Cash flow can make or break the business. One of the key lessons for O'Rourke was the importance of staying on top of receivables.

She learned a painful lesson in 2001. Her client Enron, which had become one of the world's dominant energy companies by reshaping the way natural gas and electricity are bought and sold, collapsed and filed the largest corporate bankruptcy in American history. Her accounting department was behind in billings. After the company filed for bankruptcy, O'Rourke got sixteen cents on the dollar.

She had seventy people working at Enron. While her competitors were pulling employees off the Enron business, O'Rourke refused to remove her people from the account until Enron asked them to leave, as they were overseeing the company's computer servers. "As

an infrastructure engineer, you don't leave the data until your customer tells you to leave."

According to an April 2015 Middle Market Power Index report from American Express and Dun & Bradstreet titled "Catalyzing US Economic Growth," among commercially active firms in the US, 7 percent are identified as majority women owned, and 25 percent are identified as having a female CEO. Seven percent of small firms are women owned, and 24 percent have a female CEO; 6 percent of middle-market firms are women owned, and 13 percent have a female CEO; and just 1 percent of large firms are majority women owned, with 8 percent having a female CEO.

It was almost Christmas when Enron officially shut its doors. "I didn't think I deserved to be able to enjoy Christmas since a lot of my consultants did not have a job." That experience proved to be her company's only financial loss.

While 2001 was hard, the recession that ushered in 2009 was even harder. "I went from $81.5 million to $87.5 million. That was the hardest $6 million I ever made. I had to take cuts and get new clients. That's when I started traveling more, so I could get in front of clients." O'Rourke notes that making that $6 million was harder than starting a new company.

O'Rourke has never had to worry financially and has always made money. She also maintains a good relationship with her banker. She has learned that a strong balance sheet makes for good relationships with her bankers. While she is not currently opening more offices, she has had to expand her line of credit, as her consultants' payroll is her number-one cost.

Her key takeaway from the Enron crisis and the subsequent 2008 recession was that every seven years the economy experiences a "hiccup." So you must be prepared. "You don't know what year is going to be slow. You never skate and you don't sleep, either. I don't want to fail. You have to spend the time to be successful, to make as much money as you want."

Despite the business climate, she has always given raises and Christmas bonuses to the back-office staff she calls her "backbone." "They made sure I was successful. Take care of the employees who take care of you and help you grow. You can have all the sales in the world, but if your back office is not good, you will go under."

When the market is slow, she believes that is a good time to invest in updating your technology. In that way, when the economy turns around, your infrastructure will be up to date.

O'Rourke scrutinizes accounts receivable and payable and looks at all capital expenditures. "I am the top salesperson. I stay focused on sales to grow the company. As you get larger, you depend more on your staff. The

growth of the company is the most important. The only way to grow is to get more clients to get more revenue."

When times are tough, O'Rourke says the first thing corporations put on hold is IT because that is one of the biggest expenses. So she made sure she was not concentrated in just one industry. In addition to accounting, finance, HR, and procurement, she is also in pharmaceutical, manufacturing, trash, banking, engineering, and aluminum—just about every industry except retail and government. "That has made it easy for me this year. Growth is high, considering it's been a bad year. There's an old saying that you should not put all your eggs in one basket. If you diversify, it's another way to be successful."

The one skill O'Rourke credits with fueling her fast growth is her follow-up acumen. "I don't take no for an answer. I don't give up. If they tell me no one day, then one day they will tell me yes. I will always try another way to make it happen." Whereas some entrepreneurs don't answer their phones on weekends, she is always accessible. "If a customer reaches out to me, I am there. I have always been like that. Business does not stop because I am not there. Everyone who calls always gets a live person. I don't think a customer should have to wait because I am on a plane."

In 2009, Pamela O'Rourke won the EY Entrepreneur of the Year®, Business Services for the Houston and Gulf Coast Area.

O'Rourke was a judge for the EY Entrepreneurial Winning Women program. During the program's first three years,

she was a judge and helped select the winners, before becoming one herself. "I was a tough one. Having an IT background, I am an analyst. Numbers never lie to me. I am always looking. You need to know your numbers."

Other CEOs she met through her membership in the Women Presidents' Organization still mean a great deal to her. "It's great because you have someone you can talk to, to bounce things off of. We all help each other."

TIPS FROM
PAMELA
O'ROURKE

- Start with a business plan, and stay on top of it every month.
- Get firsthand experience in the industry before you open your company. You will have keen insight into how to take care of your customers and gain a better chance of being successful.
- Surround yourself with people who are smarter than you are, so you can continue your professional growth.
- Keep costs down to increase ROI as your company grows.
- Do not hire family or friends. That is a disaster waiting to happen. When it comes to money, you have no friends.
- Run the company with the highest possible ethical standards. Never lie. You will always be able to remember the truth; it's difficult to keep track of lies.
- Pay attention to branding and marketing—make sure your logo is recognizable on all promotional items, and trademark it if you can.
- Lead by example every single day. Leadership starts at the top.
- Follow up. Client relationships take years to earn. Even if there is another supplier in place, stay on it. Some people give up after one meeting. Remember, other businesses like ICON Information Consultants are ready, willing, and able to take business away from you.
- Respond to every RFP (request for proposal)—if you don't win, there will likely be another opportunity. Also, the incumbent may fail, so you may ultimately get the business even if you did not win it at first.
- Stay on top of your EBIDA (Earnings Before Interest, Depreciation, and Amortization). If you are trying to make

money off of volume, you have to do a lot of volume, which will lower your rates and ROI. An EBIDA loss can takes years to recoup. If during down times a client asks you to reduce your billing rate, compensate for the reduction by slightly increasing rates for new clients.

- Diversify your services in as many industries as possible so that you are well positioned in the event of an economic downturn.

HUMAN RESOURCES

Recruiting and retaining talent is critical to help an organization in fast-growth mode achieve its fullest potential. Three heads of 50 Fastest-Growing Women-Owned/Led Companies reflect on some of the human resources challenges they faced in the early days of developing their companies and what that looked like during times of exponential growth.

June Ressler
President and CEO
Cenergy International Services

Sonja N. Hines
President
H&S Resources Corporation

Leslie A. Firtell, Esq.
CEO
Tower Legal Solutions

CENERGY
INTERNATIONAL SERVICES

JUNE RESSLER,
PRESIDENT
AND CEO

City, State:
Houston, TX

Year Founded:
1996

Year Won 50 Fastest:
2015

Gross Revenues:
2010:	$ 99,200,251
2012:	$280,772,684
2014:	$258,796,803

Business overview:
Cenergy International Services provides energy personnel solutions: global-workforce solutions for the world's energy-industry services.

To what do you attribute your success:
"To the wonderful team that we have supporting us that gives their all each day."

Total number of employees projected for 2015:
Internal employees number approximately seventy-five, and consultants are about one thousand.

Benefits the company provides employees:

- bonuses
- health insurance
- life insurance
- 401(k)
- flex time
- telecommuting
- long-term disability

Cenergy provides a full suite of workforce solutions globally to industries, including energy, engineering and construction, aerospace and defense, shipbuilding, and power and utilities. These solutions encompass specialized energy personnel, safety solutions, assessments and training, inspection solutions, logistics optimization, and vendor management.

With offices spanning the world (including United States, Canada, Netherlands, Scotland, and Australia), Cenergy is also supported by regional offices, as well as by a network of consultants working in some of the most remote locations on the planet.

IT DID NOT START OUT AS A DREAM

Unlike some entrepreneurs, starting a company was not June Ressler's dream. She was a practicing attorney in Pennsylvania, where she had lived for forty years, before moving to New Orleans. With three small children, she wanted to find work she could do from home to make a little extra money.

Surrounded by the thriving oil and energy field in New Orleans, Ressler decided to learn about the industry by researching what insurances were required for people

to work onsite. Talking with consultants placed offshore taught her about industry operations. Gradually, she became confident enough to start calling clients in their offices to solicit projects.

The early years were slow. Ressler never imagined owning a big company. "I was just happy keeping busy, making some money, and keeping people happy." Her business caught on in the early 2000s. After that, it was year after year of explosive growth.

GULF COAST
HURRICANE
DELIVERS HARD
LESSONS

Hurricane Katrina in 2005 brought with it some hard lessons. One of them was the importance of cloud computing. The company's computer servers were located in its New Orleans office. After Katrina pounded the Gulf Coast and the mayor shut down the city, Ressler's company was forced to evacuate its personnel to Lafayette. The computer servers were left behind. This situation seriously jeopardized a big part of what Cenergy does: paying hundreds of people on time.

"The minute we miss a paycheck our company is dead," she said. Fortuitously, one of her employees was a deputy sheriff and authorized to drive his truck into the city. He single-handedly ran up and down the company's nineteen flights of stairs, retrieving every server and delivering them all to Cenergy's Lafayette office. The company never skipped a beat. Ressler continued to pay all of her consultants, and they never knew how close she had come to not being able to pay.

Another hard lesson was the necessity of electronic banking. One of her major clients had been paying with paper checks. But post Katrina, mail could not be delivered. No one knew where the checks were going. "The mail trucks must have been floating around somewhere in the bayou with all of our checks in it. We were not receiving them, so we couldn't deposit them. We didn't get paid for one full year from one of our major clients."

BE WHERE THE BUSINESS IS

Ressler realized that if she was going to build her business quickly in the oil and energy industry, the place to be was Houston. When her lease in New Orleans was up, she moved her corporate headquarters office to Houston, and that is when she crossed over from a small business into middle-market range. "That's when we really took off. We had about thirty employees then. Now we have about eighty."

HR IS KEY TO MAINTAINING CULTURE DURING TIMES OF RAPID GROWTH

Fast growth can create a vicious cycle of staffing up quickly, then being forced to restructure six months later, then hiring and firing again. Ressler realized she could not afford the impact that a rapid personnel churn was having on her culture. "We hired people, threw them at a job, and then eventually realized they were the wrong people. It was a common theme," she said.

According to a September 2015 Middle Market Power Index report from American Express and Dun & Bradstreet titled "The Growing Economic Clout of Diverse Middle Market Firms," middle-market enterprises represent 0.7 percent of all commercially active enterprises. Firms identified as majority women owned are just as likely as average to be found in the middle market (0.7 percent), while those identified as being

majority owned by one or more minorities are more likely than average (1.6 percent) to be middle-market enterprises.

"I finally figured out that HR is a serious job," she said, "and the best decision I ever made was to hire a serious HR person to do it." She finally hired up, knowing she wanted to continue to build her company quickly. "I needed someone who could manage HR for a $500 million company, not a $250 million company. So I hired a guy that came from a billion-dollar publicly held company. He is amazing."

Cenergy – Growth over last 10 years

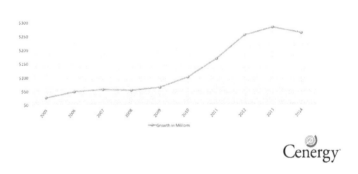

Under his leadership, Cenergy administers a written test before making a hiring decision. Ressler says if she could have done anything differently, she would have started using the test a long time ago. It has been the best investment she ever made and proved to be much more effective than the company's previous process. An HR professional can help navigate the many different employment tests and approaches available to assess knowledge, skills, and other characteristics.

"Our culture is key. We are serious about it. We expect our people to live up to the culture." Ressler is committed to excellence, providing fabulous customer service, and 360-degree accountability. "At our company, you don't check the box and say it's not my job. You own whatever you're doing, start to finish."

USE FINANCIAL INFORMATION TO MANAGE THE COMPANY

Interpreting financial information wisely is an important key to fast growth, according to Ressler, as it offers trend information gained over time, year to date compared to last year, quarterly results, and gross profits. When the oil industry felt the impact of lower prices in 2015, Ressler began doing project-based work with a more profitable model to work through the people-placement downturn.

Having an excellent banking relationship allowed Ressler to make acquisitions and other investments needed to support fast growth. She went through periods where she would grow 100 percent year after year and would run out of her line of credit, something she relied on during her periods of rapid growth to pay consultants right away. Ressler's relationship with her banker was so good she could make a call on a Friday requesting an extension on the line of credit, get verbal authorization to proceed, and then follow up on Monday with the requisite documentation.

One of the most important drivers to which she attributes her fast growth is having excellent customer service. While others give it lip service, Ressler says it is a mantra repeated over and over again at her office. "When we get opportunities, we never say no. We figure out a way to make it work."

Having a service-oriented mentality, along with a renegade attitude, is central to being successful at Cenergy. "The key is making sure your core people are solid. It's pretty rough out there. When you grow 40 percent or more, a lot of people have to spend a lot of extra time doing a lot of extra work."

Before the oil and energy industry experienced a recent downturn, Ressler started sourcing for reputable managers who were being let go to help lead her company into the growth she knew was inevitable. "I feel we are much better off because of it."

- Human resources is a serious job that can literally change the culture of an entire company. Hire someone from a company twice your size with the right credentials to oversee this important function.

- Invest in an assessment test that can be administered during the interview process.

- Secure an excellent banking relationship, as it can provide the means to do what you need to do to grow quickly.

- Identify and stick to your core values to maintain and protect your culture as you grow.

- Maintain positive energy, a commitment to excellence, and provide fabulous customer service.

- Base performance evaluations and bonuses on delivering against core values.

- Have people in different parts of the company weigh in before making a hiring decision. Involve senior leadership, administration, and marketing, at the very least.

- Acknowledge if a hire is not working out and you've provided adequate time and training.

SONJA N. HINES, PRESIDENT

City, State:
Columbia, MD

Year Founded:
2006

Year Won 50 Fastest:
2013

Gross Revenues:
2008:	$ 792,423
2010:	$ 2,595,577
2012:	$ 6,853,702

Business overview:
H&S Resources Corporation provides integrated facility and maintenance services, as well as support services in facility operations and maintenance services—including planning, consulting, HVAC (heating, ventilation, and air conditioning), plumbing, electrical, preventive maintenance, and construction—for government and commercial clients.

To what do you attribute your success:
"Our biggest breakthrough was receiving a call directly from a federal government agency requesting our capabilities. We knew the business was a winner when we secured our first federal government contract during a competitive bid."

Total number of employees: 128

Benefits provided to employees:

- health insurance
- life insurance
- 401(k)
- flex time
- car allowance/company car
- tuition reimbursement
- telecommuting
- long-term disability

YOU CAN GO HOME AGAIN

Sonja Hines did not count on having to move in with her mother and put everything she owned in storage. But when she decided to start her own company in March 2006, she had to drastically minimize her overhead.

At the time, she was working on a big government contract that would ultimately result in civilian employees losing their jobs. Even though employees had the right of first refusal before their jobs were offered to anyone else, it was a difficult time. Hines decided she had sufficient facilities-management and safety-engineering experience to go out on her own, working with a business partner, Thomas J. Scanlon, III, who specialized in construction and operations. By the end of 2007, their own company, H&S, had its first contract.

H&S is a minority woman-owned, disadvantaged small business certified 8(a) by the Small Business Administration (SBA). The company performs support services in the areas of facility operations and maintenance services, logistics operations, and construction.

Facility operations and maintenance services include planning, consulting, HVAC, plumbing, electrical, preventive maintenance, and other facility-engineering services to government agencies and commercial clients. Logistics operations run the gamut, from warehousing to traffic management to alongside aircraft refueling. H&S also offers a variety of technical and administrative services to assist in the development, management, and administration of multiple programs.

Hines started receiving requests to write proposals for larger facilities-management companies. Because this required highly specialized knowledge, she and her partner were soon considered subject-matter experts. This allowed them to develop the "seed money" required to start their own firm.

Hines received her SBA certification after less than a year of being in business because she was able to demonstrate that the company was sustainable. She was catapulted into being eligible for government contracts. The company crossed into midmarket range, generating more than $10 million in revenue in 2013, and jumping very quickly in a year and a half from thirty-two employees to 110. Now she has close to two hundred employees and is generating more than $13 million in revenue.

Hines had an ambitious, if not aggressive, goal to grow the company by 20 percent each year. Initially, she focused only on revenue and the amount of money needed to achieve that goal. As she became savvier, she focused on equity and how much profit she was making. Having a deeper understanding of financials, as opposed to how much money she was going to make, helped her to make better business decisions.

In the early days, one of Hines's biggest hurdles was the lack of financial resources. She got through this by conserving finances, downsizing, and making the decision to move in with her mother. She thoroughly educated herself on how government contracting works.

"When we take on additional work, we are always concerned about startup costs. If I take on a large job, what are the cost implications? Am I going to have to start it with $100K, $200K? Am I going to have to buy vehicles, invest in equipment?" She tried to build in flexibility by maintaining a financial cushion and keeping an ample credit line.

Having a great relationship with her banker was critical to Sonja's fast growth. "I typically tell them what we are going to bid on, especially if it's a particularly large contract, and what we will need to be successful if we win. That has helped a lot."

Hines makes her bankers part of the process after she has crunched the numbers and is about to submit her proposal, projecting potential annual revenue and what it will look like over five years.

Another approach to which she attributes fast growth is making strategic partnerships with other companies similar in scope to compete for work she could not handle on her own. "Teaming enables you to go after work that you would not ordinarily be able to pursue. Partnering and collaborating with other companies has helped us grow tremendously."

Hines has many employees located in various states. Dealing with personnel issues was one of her biggest hurdles, including contending with personal and family issues that spill over into the workplace. She has brought in HR consultants to educate and train employees in the field and managers in the corporate office, using attorneys as mediators who understand the human aspect of work.

"Some of the issues we've faced with regard to HR have been totally out in left field. I don't know how we could have been prepared for that."

One of the worst HR decisions she ever made was hiring someone and not verifying the skill set. It took a long time to correct the situation. "That hurt us financially, in terms of growth, particularly since the position was about business development. That person was the gate-keeper, and that area remained stagnant since we did not bring in anything new."

Paradoxically, one of the most successful hires she ever made was not based on previous experience. "We hired someone who had been through an unfortunate circum-stance, who was talented and needed a job. He had the ability to see my vision, where I wanted to grow, and how

to get there. Sometimes drive and passion can outweigh skill set."

To avoid making a hiring mistake, she urges bringing in professionals to develop a consistent HR program. Hines stresses a need to understand what the laws are. She adds the importance of bringing in professionals who can mitigate potential lawsuits or address negativity associated with a disgruntled employee. Use real job scenarios. When hiring an employee to write proposals, for example, first assign a project to demonstrate their skill set.

Hines describes her company's culture as a learning environment, characterized by teamwork and giving back to the community. She believes what attracts people to her company is cross training and flex time.

"We work hard, but we offer flexibility. That's what keeps people here. We allow them time to take off to receive certification and additional training to help them grow professionally. I want to make sure that should something go awry, you have enough under your belt that you can take it with you and go to another job. Continue your professional development. Seek certification if you want, or if there is a seminar you want to attend, go for it. I think that's a very attractive proposition."

The top three core attributes for candidates to be successful in her company are:

- Strong communications skills: "We are all doing so much. If we don't communicate, it's easy to misinterpret a path or miss it altogether. I need to understand what your needs are, what problems you are having, and what drives you. I encourage

open communication, either face-to-face, by phone, or email. I know this is sometimes easier said than done."

- Endurance: With extremely long days, endurance is critical. Deadlines mean all hands on deck, and people need to be able to keep going.

- Flexibility: Being flexible is also crucial. "Sometimes we go down one path and end up having to make a U-turn."

Hines advises other middle-market company leaders to identify the right team players to help their companies scale. "You don't always get it right the first time. It takes a while to find the right players, and it generally goes back to the hiring and firing process. You need to do it the right way. Once you have that team, you will be amazed at what you can accomplish. Growing a company is a team effort. You don't do it by yourself."

TIPS FROM
SONJA N. HINES

- Make sure you thoroughly understand your company's financials and have the appropriate "back office" infrastructure in place to be able to grow.

- Have experts in place to deal with HR, legal, and financial issues.

- Be strategic. Consider partnering with other companies to increase your reach and scope.

- Be slow to hire—it's important to have the right people in the right roles.

- Recognize when it's not the right fit, and take action as soon as possible.

- Understand what the HR laws are and the best way to terminate.

- Bring in an outside professional who can advise and preventatively navigate situations.

- Verify employees have the skills they say they have before hiring.

- Have a plan in place to address potential legal issues.

TOWER LEGAL SOLUTIONS

LESLIE FIRTELL,
CEO

City, State:
New York, NY

Year Founded:
2007

Year Won 50 Fastest:
2015

Gross Revenues:
2010:	$ 14,047,935
2012:	$ 56,396,938
2014:	$ 59,488,380

Business overview:
Tower Legal Solutions provides full-service legal staffing, compliance, and managed-review solutions.

To what do you attribute your success:
"Don't be afraid to take risks. I hire, and I constantly reinvest in the company to make it bigger, better, and stronger."

Total number of employees: 70

Benefits they provide employees:

- bonuses

- health insurance

- 401(k)

- tuition reimbursement

When someone asked Leslie Firtell why her employees looked so happy, she knew it was because culture has been paramount in her firm's fast growth.

A full-service legal staffing and managed legal-review company, Tower Legal Solutions focuses on reducing risk and controlling discovery costs, as well as making the best possible match in legal staffing—from temporary to temp-to-hire or direct hire.

Having once been a successful lawyer and salesperson in charge of business development and recruiting, Firtell was unexpectedly terminated. While competitors probed her interest in working for them, she took a chance and went out on her own. Investing $354,000 of her own money, she opened an office with 4,200 square feet in downtown Manhattan, paying six months rent in advance to secure the lease. Eight years later, she is still in the same building, with thirty thousand square feet, occupying the entire thirteenth floor, half of the seventeenth floor, and a portion of the eighteenth floor. She also has six offices nationwide and seventy employees.

According to a September 2015 Middle Market Power Index report from American Express and Dun & Bradstreet titled "The Growing Economic Clout of Diverse Middle Market Firms," women-owned and minority-owned firms are moving into the middle market (between $10 million and $1 billion in revenues) at an impressive pace and are playing a vital role in the American economy, driving revenue and employment growth among this population. In fact, women and minorities are entering into the middle

market at rates five to seven times the rate of all commercially active businesses. Between 2008 and 2014, the number of women-owned or led firms in the middle market has increased by 32.4 percent, and the number of majority women-owned firms in the middle market has increased by 23.6 percent.

DIVERSIFICATION CAN SPUR FAST GROWTH

While Firtell's firm had a very successful first year, billing $20 million, her two largest clients—Bear Stearns and Merrill Lynch—went out of business shortly thereafter. She had to rebuild. Although business dipped in years three and four, it then grew to $39 million, climbed to $56 million, hit $83 million, and then dropped to $62 million.

When Firtell started, she was purely a temporary legal-staffing company. One of the unanticipated pitfalls was loss of clients due to marketplace volatility. This inspired her to diversify her business model to offer more than one product area. When the economy improves, there is less litigation that requires temporary legal staffing. Now Firtell also does compliance, contract manage-ment, and legal consulting and has a permanent staffing division.

INVEST IN BRINGING THE RIGHT PEOPLE ON BOARD

In 2015, Firtell celebrated her eighth year in business. For the first two years, she never took a salary, opting to reinvest in her company instead. From early on she focused on bringing the right people on board. She urges CEOs or key decision makers at middle-market companies not to be afraid to invest in higher-salary/higher-skilled people because they will help you to scale up and increase your revenue even more. "You also don't want to spend your

entire day micromanaging people, because your time must be devoted to focusing on the business."

When Firtell first learned of the person who is currently her COO, she said she could not afford the salary. "I almost choked but my accountant told me that when the time is right it will be the best investment that I could make." When she was ready, she realized the investment was well worth it.

"When you first open a business, you hire what you can afford, and you hope for the best. But when you get to a place where you've developed a reputation and have reached a certain level, talent starts coming to you, and you can afford to hire more experienced people."

One of the ways in which she fueled fast growth was by opening satellite offices in lower-cost markets. Charlotte, Dallas, and Minneapolis offered cost-effective options to supplement outside counsel in order to keep expenses down. This gave clients an added incentive to begin working with her company. As a result, the volume of work she received increased, while the cost to her clients went down.

Firtell has built customer loyalty through an unwavering focus on quality, integrity, cost-effective processes, and superior service. Growing her organization has been closely linked with how she managed her human resources. The culture Firtell envisioned was one of respect, humility, trust, and kindness.

Firtell believes the top three attributes for an employee to be successful in her company are being respectful,

providing good customer service, and being an entrepreneurial thinker. One of the most important attributes to which she attributes her fast growth is customer service. "Around 80 percent of business is repeat business," she said. "We were obviously doing something right as we focused on delivering the unexpected."

My Story, Our Story

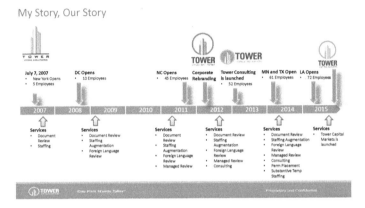

Firtell credits peer-learning organizations like the Women Presidents' Organization with fueling her fast growth. "I could not have done it myself. Since I opened my company in 2007, I have always been part of the Women Presidents' Organization. I am in three chapters—local New York, Platinum, and Zenith."[2] She is also the only WPO Legacy member. Her mother had a courier business and was part of the first chapter when the organization opened in 1997. Firtell is also in EY Entrepreneurial Winning Women.

Looking back on her rapid-growth trajectory, Firtell doesn't think she would have done anything differently. "I took the risks, and they more or less ended up being the right moves. Even though I was never very good at it, I learned how to delegate."

[2] WPO Platinum level members have gross revenues over $10 million annually; average revenue is $42 million. Zenith level gross revenue is over $50 million annually; average revenue is $100 million.

Successful placements require particular interpersonal team dynamics, in addition to expertise. Firtell recognizes the value of HR analytics and uses a thorough, behavioral-based interview process to select candidates that offer the best fit for each position. She evaluates candidates based on six core characteristics:

- adaptability
- ambition
- leadership
- self-assessment
- stress management
- teamwork

"My biggest lesson was that it's 100 percent okay to hire people who are more skilled in their area than you are. You don't have to have all the answers. And I do not."

- Do not be afraid to take risks. Firtell took them, and they ended up being the right moves.

- Think and act big.

- Learn the difference between leading and managing, and learn how to delegate.

- Reinvest in your company to make it bigger, better, and stronger.

- Invest in higher-salary/higher-skilled people. It will help you make even more money in the long run.

- Provide amazing customer service: 80 percent of Firtell's business is repeat business.

- Always stay ahead of the curve: don't be so far behind you can't catch up.

- Focus on delivering the unexpected: don't overpromise and underdeliver.

- Create a culture of respect and success. While there will be pitfalls, your culture must remain constant. Figure out how to keep it growing when you are adding staff from different companies.

INNOVATION

Effective leaders grasp the notion that encouraging their employees to seek new perspectives and contribute innovative ideas are powerful drivers of fast growth. Three of the 50 Fastest-Growing Women-Owned/Led Companies reflect on the power of innovation in accelerating the growth of their companies.

Phyllis Newhouse
President and CEO
Xtreme Solutions, Inc.

Denise Wilson
President and CEO
Desert Jet

Kara trott
CEO
Quatum Health

Xtreme Solutions, Inc.
Solving the World's Problems with Xtreme Solutions!

XTREME SOLUTIONS, INC.

PHYLLIS NEWHOUSE,
PRESIDENT
AND CEO

City, State:
Atlanta, GA

Year Founded:
2002

Year Won 50 Fastest:
2015

Gross Revenues:
2010: $ 3,674,570
2012: $ 7,922,291
2014: $ 36,641,740

Business overview:
Xtreme Solutions combines best practices in information technology, along with key partnerships with many of the top security-solutions manufacturers, to provide federal agencies and major corporations with superior information technology (IT) and cybersecurity solutions. Utilizing the latest technologies and dedicated security experts, Xtreme Solutions is able to provide services that protect its clients against foreign and domestic cybersecurity threats.

To what do you attribute your success:
"I attribute leadership to success. I also know that having a great team of leaders has attributed to success of the business."

After spending twenty-two years in the military, Phyllis Newhouse knew the federal government was outsourcing the majority of its IT services. Before she left military service in 1999, Newhouse began to formulate a way to leverage the leadership acumen and skill set she had gained to build an IT company with the "right stuff" to pitch to the Department of Defense. The company was up and running by 2002.

Newhouse's pivotal make-or-break moment came in 2005, when she bid on a large government contract. Despite having minimal resources and very little operating capital, she won the contract based on what she believes was trust in her ability to do the job.

On a Saturday afternoon, she got a telephone call from a contract officer who said she was happy that Xtreme Solutions had won the business. "She said it was the first time she had the pleasure of awarding a contract of that size to a veteran. She encouraged me to do a fantastic job because my performance would count and would open doors for other women-owned businesses."

According to a September 2015 Middle Market Power Index report from American Express and Dun & Bradstreet titled "The Growing Economic Clout of Diverse Middle Market Firms," women-owned/women-led middle-market firms in the US comprise just 0.4 percent of all women-owned or led US firms yet employ one-quarter (23 percent) of workers and contribute one-quarter (25 percent) of the revenues accounted for by all women-owned/women-led firms. With respect to the minority-owned firm popu-

lation, middle-market firms represent 1.6 percent of all minority-owned firms yet employ more than one third (34 percent) of the workers and generate fully 42 percent of the revenues accounted for by minority-owned businesses in the US.

USING FINANCIAL INFORMATION TO MANAGE THE COMPANY

Phyllis Newhouse reached $10 million in revenue after fewer than three years in business. To this day, her company is debt free. She has never considered using factoring companies or taking on private-equity partners.

Owing to her experience in the military, Newhouse understood the logistics of the Federal Supply Service system that allows approved contractors to submit invoices quickly and efficiently. Payments are received within days, virtually eliminating any drain on cash flow. "Most people don't understand the government has a fast pay system." She used it to her advantage and negotiated payment terms upfront. Because invoices were paid in fifteen or thirty days, within sixty days she was debt free and without any excess capital fees.

Using a financial-management dashboard system she calls a smart board, Newhouse has developed a hybrid of applications from different accounting systems to provide a timely snapshot of her P&L with access to real-time data for reporting and forecasting.

THE DAY I COME TO WORK COMFORTABLE, SOMETHING IS WRONG

One of the pitfalls of growth can be growing too fast. "No one tells you to anticipate you are going to grow fast. You start having a lot of problems with scaling." Now

Newhouse uses metrics to gauge growth in advance to set up strategic-infrastructure needs.

While she did not anticipate every pitfall along the way, Newhouse was not surprised when they happened. "Having come out of the military, you are tasked with getting the mission done. You don't anticipate failing. But you may have to be flexible and have the ability to restructure how the mission is accomplished."

She does not allow success to morph into complacence. "The day I come to work comfortable, then something is wrong."

HOLDING PEOPLE ACCOUNTABLE IS KEY FOR FAST GROWTH

The Xtreme Solutions business culture is one in which fast growth is a key ingredient. Everyone is responsible for it and is encouraged to maintain an entrepreneur's mind-set.

In a fiercely competitive industry that has grown explosively in the last seven years, bringing innovative solutions to the table is critical to staying competitive. Forging strategic partnerships, particularly in data analytics, has been particularly important in accelerating growth.

A major systems breach in an aviation carrier led to the development of a program for tracking potentially suspicious packages on planes flying to countries on the interest list. The US stopped shipping packages to a particular location after the system was in place.

"As a result of that contract, the government wanted us to monitor this system from then on. Thinking outside

the box presented a great opportunity; 25 percent of our growth that year came from that one idea. That is the mind-set we all have: that one idea can cause a spike in our revenues."

Xtreme Solutions Inc. Revenue Growth

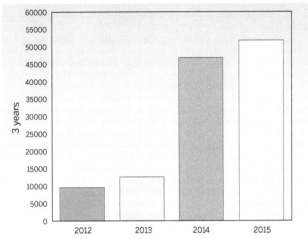

IDENTIFY SUPPORT
SYSTEMS ALONG
THE WAY

While having a mentor is important, Newhouse has surrounded herself with people she refers to as her "external think tank." They provide a sounding board she has learned to count on for valuable feedback and, most importantly, to tell her the truth. "In order to scale your business, you must have people you can reach out to and touch sometimes."

Newhouse joined the Women Presidents' Organization through the Women of Color Achievement Awards, a WPO partnership with 100 Black Men of America. The selection criteria for the award included successful operation of a woman-owned or led business that has reached annual revenues of at least $2 million for prod-uct-based businesses or $1 million for service-based businesses. Companies must also have significantly

strengthened the US economy by providing an increase in employment opportunities on a local, regional, and national level.

"My first year in WPO was a phenomenal one. Just to have a support group like that and to be engaged and listen to the thought process of other leaders opened up other opportunities. Resources I did not think were available became accessible as a result of WPO connections."

Other resources that women entrepreneurs can utilize include ChallengeHER, a partnership between the US Small Business Administration (SBA), Women Impacting Public Policy (WIPP), and American Express OPEN (OPEN), which works to strengthen and promote the Women-Owned Small Business (WOSB) Federal Contract Program. ChallengeHER launched in Washington, DC, in April 2013 with government officials, contracting experts, and women contractors. Its goal was to boost government contracting opportunities for women-owned small businesses. The program provides women entrepreneurs across the country with the knowledge, tools, and connections needed to compete successfully in the government marketplace.

While in WPO, Newhouse was nominated for the EY Entrepreneurial Winning Women program, which escalated opportunities for business exposure. From a marketing and branding perspective, getting her company broad-based exposure to provide commentary on cybersecurity issues greatly enhanced its visibility and was a critical component of its growth.

Newhouse believes that no matter what stage of success a business has achieved, resources are available to scale or sustain growth. "I became a big advocate of women getting involved in these organizations earlier, when they hit the million-dollar mark in business and they feel they are at the point of scalability. I preach this to a lot of women—that they have to get involved— because of what WPO has done for me."

A COMPANY DEFINED BY CUTTING-EDGE TECHNOLOGY

As an ethical-hacking firm, Xtreme Solutions helps identify potential threats on a computer or network by searching the system for weak points that could be exploited. So it is critical that the company remain highly innovative in the kinds of solutions it brings to its customers, offering mitigating strategies that prevent a breach from happening.

Innovation can sometimes mean aligning with other companies and forging strategic partnerships, blending two core competencies to create one distinctive solution.

The company is working on cobranding an initiative offering predictive analysis and big data. Using this intelligence platform, all major airline carriers would have the ability to track every package brought onto a plane, all over the world. The predictive-analysis tool delivers a robust real-time analysis, significantly reducing the time it takes the federal government and foreign agencies to do the requisite analytics. A process that used to take six months, the predictive analysis and cybersharing can now be accomplished within minutes of an inquiry. A digital forensic-alert system is also underway to alert first responders during a disaster.

Another innovative application underway designed to address the chaos surrounding the first critical moments after a big disaster is a digital forensic-alert system. Currently in beta testing, it pinpoints the exact origin to quickly and efficiently deploy first responders.

INNOVATIVE
APPROACH TO
ADDRESSING
THE ISSUE OF
CAPACITY

Due to the wildly escalating volume, complexity, and scale of cybersecurity breaches today, one of Newhouse's biggest challenges has been finding experienced cyberexperts who are also officially certified. Certification involves passing a very complex and expensive test. "We found that the failure rate was about 74 percent for the first-time tester. So we decided to build our own cyberacademy."

Xtreme Solutions built a learning-management tool and now offers cybertraining to experts all over the world. Applicants have the opportunity to tap into a virtual lab and test their skill set before taking the test. The failure rate plummeted from 74 percent to 4.5 percent.

The company not only trained and hired these officially certified experts, but they also offered a pool of approved talent back to the industry. The cybertraining project created an additional revenue stream. "We went online eight months ago and are already generating $4.5 million in revenue."

ENCOURAGING
INNOVATIVE
THINKING

Unlike some leaders, Newhouse does not give her employees permission to fail as a way to encourage innovative thinking. "You can't tell a soldier it is okay to fail, as it could cause loss of life." Rather, she views failure as an opportunity to correct the process and to document what went wrong.

Having seen that fast-growth companies allow people to be innovative in how they think, particularly the younger members of the work force, the company sponsors four think-tank days each year. Employees pitch their ideas, and if the company implements them, the employee shares the revenue.

One of the most innovative ideas to accelerate the growth of Newhouse's company was the development of the counterintelligence platform solution. "We are now known for this operational-intelligence platform that can give you real-time cyberoperational intelligence from a network perspective. Moving to that level was very innovative and caused us to have accelerated growth. We were able to land big contracts with the federal government and the defense department. That was huge for us."

INNOVATION SAYS A LOT ABOUT THE CALIBER OF NEW BUSINESS INQUIRIES

Maintaining quality and innovation has enabled Xtreme Solutions to be considered a subject-matter expert and a trusted "go-to" partner. The company doesn't solicit business. "We have received a phone call after a major disaster happens internationally to get someone to FBI headquarters in Washington, DC, to support them on some digital forensics and cyberoperations needs when they don't have the resources."

Newhouse finds that one of her business challenges continues to be that people do not understand the complexity of cyberbreaches and resist upgrading their systems until there is a problem. "We tend to sell from an offensive versus defensive perspective." It is a mind-set change to proactively invest in preventing an attack rather than defend one taking place.

"Some people in the C-suite don't understand how innovation can help their bottom line and mitigate strategies to prevent a loss of revenue."

TIPS FROM
PHYLLIS
NEWHOUSE

- Research the availability and logistics of quick-pay systems with government contracts.

- Anticipate fast growth by putting metrics in place in advance to gauge growth and to set up strategic infrastructure needs.

- Do not allow success to morph into complacency.

- Have an external think tank as a sounding board you can count on to provide valuable feedback and, most importantly, to tell you the truth.

- Make everyone responsible for the company's growth, and encourage them to have an entrepreneur's mind-set.

- Forge strategic partnerships to bring innovative solutions to the table, stay competitive, and accelerate growth.

- Become an expert on issues surrounding your company's core competency to enhance visibility for your expertise.

- Identify professional support systems, like the Women Presidents' Organization, to make incremental resources available and accessible as a result of shared connections.

- Invest proactively in preventing a cyberattack before it happens rather than defend one taking place. Mitigate from a loss of revenue, and protect your bottom line.

DESERT JET

DENISE WILSON,
PRESIDENT
AND CEO

City, State:
Thermal, CA

Year Founded:
2007

Year Won 50 Fastest:
2014

Gross Revenues:
2009: $ 849,643
2011: $ 4,971,510
2013: $ 8,752,083

Business overview:
Desert Jet is a group of aircraft charter, maintenance, and executive aircraft-handling companies headquartered in Palm Springs, California. Founded by pilot and entrepreneur Denise Wilson, Desert Jet operates a fleet of nine jet aircraft based throughout Southern California.

To what do you attribute your success:
"I have always had the drive to be the best at whatever I am doing. I don't let unfamiliarity stop me from doing everything I can to learn a new subject. I say yes, then figure it out later."

HOW DO YOU GET TO CARNEGIE HALL?

Denise Wilson was studying to be a classical musician when she decided to take flying lessons as a hobby.

Her avocation took center stage, and she enjoyed it so much that she changed careers. Denise worked for Aloha Airlines before the company folded. She was then flying privately and started her own business in 2007. From there, her company literally took off.

Denise quickly saw the value in providing the services her company offers. Traveling by aircraft charter is one of the quickest and most convenient ways to travel. More than five thousand airports are available to charter flights nationwide, compared to only five hundred airports used by commercial airlines.

Another advantage is that you can immediately board the aircraft with no delays upon arrival at the airport, and you avoid connecting flights, as well as any worries about lost luggage. Chartering a jet increases efficiency by enabling clients to make multiple visits to clients in different cities and return the same day. Pets can fly in the cabin with you and can sit on your lap without a carrier.

"People make one phone call, and we dispatch an aircraft like you would a private car. It's a very simple process." Her maintenance company services private jets, and she assists customers who fly often and decide that having their own plane makes sense with sales and acquisition of jet aircraft.

INEXPERIENCE IS NOT NECESSARILY INABILITY

Because Wilson was a musician before she started her business as a pilot and had no business experience, she didn't anticipate many of the pitfalls to beginning her own company. Starting a business was a learning experience from day one. "I am an avid reader, so as I

started the business, I basically read every book I could find on how to start, grow, and scale a business. I went to conferences. I just learned from the sources I had available to me."

Using a variety of resources has helped get her up to speed on being a business owner, including participation in The EY Entrepreneurial Winning Women program. "They do a great job of putting women together with similar aspirations and challenges and get you to think big. You work on the business rather than in it. It has helped me see other successful women as mentors and think about where I can take my business. I see a much larger company than I thought we would be."

When Wilson joined the Women Presidents' Organization, there was no chapter located near her, so she joined the Platinum Chapter (gross revenue over $10 million annually). "I have been able to get to conferences, see great speakers, and meet women in a wider net of industries."

UNIQUE SALES PROPOSITION

The company's unique sales proposition is simple: responsiveness and speed. While it may seem counterintuitive, every member of the team—from the dispatcher to the owner of the company—is available to

take calls and answer questions or concerns. "We are the only company in the industry that you can call and we will answer the phone 24/7. Responsiveness is our biggest draw. We can have an airplane ready for you in two hours."

"Our pilots are the cornerstone of our company, so we hire only the best. Our pilots are the most highly compensated in the industry, ensuring we attract only the best and brightest flight crews."

FAST GROWTH ATTRIBUTED TO LISTENING TO TRAVEL "PAIN POINTS"

Built around what the busy person needs, using private aircraft is an effective way for people to be as productive as possible when traveling. Wilson's biggest competition is other companies that offer fractional ownership where you buy a share of an aircraft or those that offer investing in a jet card where you pay in advance for one hundred to two hundred hours of flight.

One of the most innovative things she has done to accelerate the growth of her company is to remove the roadblocks from the process of booking a private jet. For instance, clients who are repeat users sign a contract for the first flight, and the next time, all they have to do is book a flight.

"We also answer our phones, which sounds simple but is not common in our industry. We have invested a lot in people to answer the phone so that they can walk you through the process of booking a private jet."

LIMITED ABILITY TO BE INNOVATIVE

The ability to be innovative in Wilson's business is somewhat restricted, as it is not possible to build a more technologically advanced aircraft or to revolu-

tionize the private-aviation industry. One organization is assembling a unified database of aircraft that will make booking a private plane as easy as booking an airline ticket.

"It's hard for a small company like us to effect change with the regulatory requirements we have. The things we can control are culture and customer service." Desert Jet has been on the forefront of trying to remove barriers and make it an easy process to use business aviation. "People don't understand how to do it. We are trying to make that process easy, transparent, and accessible."

The marketing is largely grass roots. There is no advertising. Customers are attracted primarily by word of mouth: people tell their friends about the great service they've received.

As a fast-growth company, one of the biggest challenges is capacity. Onboarding is one of the most important processes; training is constant. New employees are assigned a mentor who works with them for a forty-five-day period called "boot camp." Employees meet one-on-one with their supervisor once a week to talk about what they are struggling with so that they can be integrated into the team environment. If they are not the right fit with the culture or company values, it quickly becomes apparent.

"I use the word 'cult' in a good way. Our employees are fiercely protective of our culture. Everyone interviews new candidates and gives a thumbs up or down."

Everyone is vigilant about living the company's values. When someone is caught in the act doing so, they receive a gift card and a complimentary email. One of Desert Jet's values is "give them the wow." That applies to both customers and fellow employees. When a flight crew was flying a team to celebrate its fire academy graduation, they distributed red plastic fireman hats. An email went out congratulating the crew for being creative and giving passengers the "wow."

"It's a visible reinforcement of values. Everyone sees that going above and beyond. That motivates everyone's game. It also provides ideas on how to put our company values into action."

Another value is to be "extraordinary together." "I have not learned by succeeding time after time. It was by falling on my face, making the wrong turn in many areas that helped me learn a critical lesson, to make me do better in the next stage."

Other values:

- Safety is paramount in an aviation company.
- Be extraordinary together, and reach for operational excellence, knowing it is not a perfect state but rather a process of trying to be better.
- Improve something today.
- See it through and be accountable.
- Help from the heart, and share business-aviation values to the community through volunteerism.

Desert Jet makes it a point to partner with other organizations to coordinate free flights for compassionate reasons, including pet rescue, transporting people with

compromised immune systems to cancer treatments, sending kids with medical needs to camps—places they would not be able to go without being flown there.

Several years ago, Wilson noticed that a lot of people were being stranded in the desert because of aircraft mechanical issues and regularly had to call a maintenance team four hours away in Los Angeles to do repairs. This was causing numerous delays. Wilson started a maintenance company to address this need. She now has a fast-growing jet maintenance company with two rescue vehicles—an airplane and a van—to assist jets when they have a last-minute mechanical emergency.

The private-aviation industry has a lot of new entrants from companies with venture capital money. Along with the infusion of cash come a variety of new ideas to reduce the price of private aviation service so that clients get used to a lower cost. That is a challenge for everyone. "We know what things cost. When you cut costs, you cut safety. We have seen many great ideas executed that we know are not sustainable. If you can't at least break even, there is no point in doing it."

- Learn from every resource available to you on how to start, grow, and scale a business. Books and conferences offer valuable information baselines.

- Join membership organizations for exposure to other successful women as role models for where you can take your business.

- Have a unique sales proposition: focus on responsiveness and speed.

- Hire the best and brightest talent you can afford.

 WOMEN PRESIDENTS' ORGANIZATION. Reaching Farther. Together.   WPO 50 Fastest Growing Women-Owned/Led Companies Guide to Growth Sponsored by American Express

113

- Focus on what you can control, such as culture and customer service.

- Remember that word-of-mouth endorsements are the most powerful marketing mechanisms. People tell their friends about the great service they've received.

- Keep a constant focus on training. As a fast-growth company, one of the biggest challenges is capacity, and employee onboarding is one of the most important processes.

- Be vigilant about living the company values.

- Reinforce the importance of living company values and putting them into action to motivate everyone to up their game.

- Be extraordinary together.

- Address a marketplace need as a way to expand your business.

QUANTUM HEALTH

KARA TROTT,
CEO

City, State:
Columbus, OH

Year Founded:
1999

Year Won 50 Fastest:
2015

Goss Revenues:
2010: $ 13,343,081
2012: $ 33,628,178
2014: $ 40,111,928

Business overview:
Quantum Health is the leading care-coordination and consumer-navigation company, serving the needs of self-insured public and private employers across the United States. With a background in consumer behavior and a deep understanding of how real people experience healthcare, Quantum Health has a proven history of improving the efficiency of clients' benefits plans while maintaining industry-leading satisfaction rates and claims savings.

To what do you attribute your success:
"We provide a customer experience that is unsurpassed in an industry where consumer trust is very low. We have intentionally built a culture and business model that sustains our ability to continue to deliver such results.

We have a leadership focus that is other centered, and all of our executives exhibit authenticity, vision, integrity, and humility, and we are able to get the best out of our people."

Kara Trott leveraged her background in consumer research to gain keen insight into the kind of "journey" an individual experiences when going through a health-care event. Then she built a company focused on delivering exactly what the consumer wanted.

For consumers, the health-care journey is often fraught with confusion, frustration, and fear. Many decisions must be made but with little support. Because the system befuddles both patients and providers, they do not use it in the most efficient manner, and wasteful spending occurs.

Experts estimate that 30–40 percent of all medical events are unnecessary. By helping patients to understand and use their benefits more efficiently, Quantum Health reduces health-care confusion.

Kara Trott created a program, grounded in consumer research, that reorganizes benefits delivered through the complex health-care system. Executed through the employer's benefit plan, the program reduces cost and empowers smarter decision making.

Founded in 1999, Quantum Health is considered a "disruptive innovation" in what industry analysts describe as a "white-hot" health-care benefit space. Companies hire Quantum to work directly with the people covered under their health plans.

Trott's clients, who typically have five thousand or more employees, self-fund their benefits and use carriers for claim payment and networks.

Trott's professional odyssey began in the consumer goods and services industries, working on consumer intercept strategies for major brands informed by large-scale market-research projects. The experiential research methodology offered a way of metaphorically standing in the consumer's shoes to gain a deeper understanding of what their personal experience with the brand looked and felt like. Based on those findings, she reoriented product distribution, store design, and retail services to match up to that natural experience.

After earning her law degree, Trott was tasked with building the consulting subsidiary of her law firm's health-care advisory practice. Based on experience in other industries, Trott identified an opportunity. Using the same methodology she had employed in goods and services resulted in a 20 percent increase in revenue or market share for her firm. Theorizing the same would hold true for health care, she proposed a study.

"At the end of the study I hypothesized that if you can understand and map out the consumer journey during a health-care experience and understand how patients showed up and what happened to them, how they made decisions, how issues came together, and where the disconnect happened, you could design a better approach to creating that guidance and support."

While the firm gave her access to its clients, it did not support the initiative, believing it would not generate

sufficient fees. So Trott put theory into practice and created her own company to drive her hypothesis forward.

According to a April 2015 Middle Market Power Index report from American Express and Dun & Bradstreet titled "Catalyzing US Economic Growth," middle-market firms make an outsized contribution to the US economy. While representing less than 1 percent of US businesses, they account for 21 percent of business revenues and employ 28 percent of the private-sector workforce nationwide. As of 2014, they number more than 136,000, employ more than fifty million workers, and generate nearly $6.2 trillion in revenues.

USING FINANCIAL INFORMATION TO MANAGE THE COMPANY

One of Quantum's first angel investors had been an advisor to large private-equity funds. In the early years, he helped Kara come up with the financial discipline to make the requisite cash flow. "When I started the company, the burn rate was about $40K per month." By 2001, the company was profitable.

Because Trott did not want to turn decision-making control over to someone else, she decided to accept a lower rate of EBIDA (Earnings Before Interest, Depreciation, and Amortization).

"I did not want any one client to be more than 20 percent of the business or to be forced to take outside money to fund operations or growth. We have maintained a disciplined financial approach to growth, ensuring our growth would be able to be internally financed while

producing a modest EBIDA. In our analysis, we are able to sustain a growth rate of 100 percent per year without outstripping our cash. This allows us to choose whether we bring in any outside investors and, if so, to name our terms. We have always been courted by private-equity firms."

While the size of her base has increased significantly, she has continued to maintain a 40 percent annual growth rate.

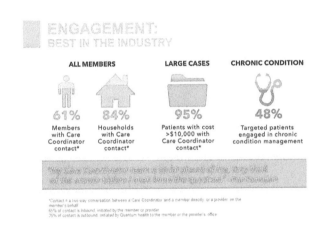

ENGAGEMENT:
BEST IN THE INDUSTRY

	ALL MEMBERS		LARGE CASES	CHRONIC CONDITION
	61%	84%	95%	48%
	Members with Care Coordinator contact*	Households with Care Coordinator contact*	Patients with cost >$10,000 with Care Coordinator contact*	Targeted patients engaged in chronic condition management

"My Care Coordinator team is so far ahead of me, they think of the answer before I even know the question." —Plan Enrollee

*Contact = a two-way conversation between a Care Coordinator and a member directly, or a provider, on the member's behalf.
65% of contact is inbound, initiated by the member or provider.
35% of contact is outbound, initiated by Quantum health to the member or the provider's office.

STRATEGIC APPROACH TO GROWTH

Given the structure of the industry, the small number of health-care carriers who have remained in business have a vested interest in maintaining the status quo. "For our approach to work, you need to shut down many of the services they provide to employers which don't create the same value that we create. We knew if we went to large companies as a starting point for our services, with no track record of results, we would not be likely to generate business."

She started midmarket, targeting companies with five hundred to one thousand employees. "We needed several years of experience across different industries

WOMEN PRESIDENTS'
ORGANIZATION.
Reaching Farther. Together.

and benefit designs, demographics, and geographic locations in order to prove what we did was replicable."

By 2006, Trott had sufficient basis for validation. In 2007, the results were in. "We had to have all our ducks in a row with proven value before we went to the real target market, which is more than five thousand employees." She began marketing to larger companies and the company is now ten times the size it was in 2008.

DON'T LOOK TO YOUR COMPANY FOR YOUR JOB

Trott refers to her company as a "project" and has never looked to the company for her job. "I have seen people get stuck when their business grows and their role changes. You begin as chief cook and bottle washer and then have to turn things over and develop a real leadership team, not just a management team."

She believes the biggest challenge is to be what the organization needs you to be, not what you enjoy or want. It is a hard thing to get used to if you are used to gauging the success of your performance on being productive.

"You have to have strong self-management skills and look at your role as pulling the best out of others. You should be interested in others, not be interesting to them. It's not about you; it's about everyone else."

SCALING A BUSINESS FOR GROWTH

Results show that if you treat every member like a friend, and not just a file number, you improve outcomes, experience, and the bottom line. "Culture is intentional and changes over time. You have to define the core elements of the culture that are contributing to your

business. The way you achieve culture may change, but you need to hardwire your three to four guiding principles into the organization."

Quantum Health's care coordinators are a resourceful and highly responsive team of nurses, social workers, and patient-service representatives and benefits experts. They are trained to be empathetic on the one hand but critical thinkers and decision makers on the other. As they are listening and figuring out what the problem is, they are empowered to make decisions and have the authority to act on them.

By overseeing all aspects of benefit delivery, the care coordinators can intercept redundant, delayed, and questionable treatment, literally driving unnecessary medical events and costs out of the system.

The company has a quirky culture (employees can choose to wear pajamas to the office), but it is coupled with the expectation to exercise the freedom they experience in the workplace in a way that supports the mission and is appropriate for the member.

The company's culture is governed by I CARE values:

C = Caring: I am passionate about helping people.

A = Accountable: I am reliable; you can count on me to give my best effort every day.

R = Real: I am genuine; I speak with good purpose and act with integrity.

E = Envelopes: I help stuff 'em.

REDUCING COST
FOR CLIENTS
SPURS FAST
GROWTH

Quantum Health competes in an environment where it is urgent for employers to find ways to reduce health-care costs. "Validated studies show we consistently reduce costs by 6.6 percent the first year, then 20 percent each year thereafter. That is a huge attraction."

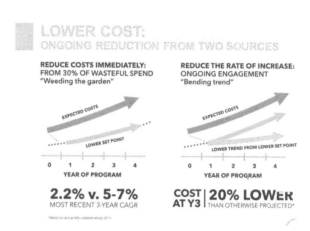

LOWER COST:
ONGOING REDUCTION FROM TWO SOURCES

REDUCE COSTS IMMEDIATELY: FROM 30% OF WASTEFUL SPEND "Weeding the garden"

REDUCE THE RATE OF INCREASE: ONGOING ENGAGEMENT "Bending trend"

EXPECTED COSTS
LOWER SET POINT
0 1 2 3 4
YEAR OF PROGRAM

EXPECTED COSTS
LOWER TREND FROM LOWER SET POINT
0 1 2 3 4
YEAR OF PROGRAM

2.2% v. 5-7% MOST RECENT 3-YEAR CAGR

COST AT Y3 | **20% LOWER** THAN OTHERWISE PROJECTED*

Trott's company is ranked by net-promoter score (NPS), which measures consumer satisfaction. Clients rate Quantum at plus seventy NPS—many times higher than her competition. "That is a huge differentiator for our clients who are looking to retain and recruit talent. The combination is that we produce results in a way that equates with superior experience." Operating in a market with significant urgency to deliver health-care benefits better and more efficiently has enabled her to grab opportunities for rapid growth.

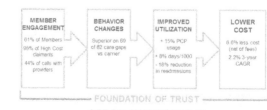

ENGAGEMENT DRIVES ALL RESULTS

MEMBER ENGAGEMENT	BEHAVIOR CHANGES	IMPROVED UTILIZATION	LOWER COST
81% of Members 98% of High Cost claimants 44% of calls with providers	Superior on 69 of 82 care gaps vs carrier	+ 15% PCP usage + 8% days/1000 - 18% reduction in readmissions	6.6% less cost (net of fees) 2.2% 3-year CAGR

FOUNDATION OF TRUST
NPS OF +70 VS CARRIER -20

- Do not get stuck when your business grows and your role changes. Learn how to turn things over, and develop a real leadership team.

- Be what your organization needs you to be, not what you enjoy being or want to be.

- Know that your strength is the vision.

- Hire people who know more than you do.

- Look at your role as pulling the best out of others.

- Focus on being interested in others, not on being interesting to them. It's not about you; it's about everyone else.

- Define the core elements of the culture that are contributing to your business.

- Hardwire your three to four guiding principles into the organization.

- Produce results in a way that equates with superior customer service.

SALES

Companies need to implement the right strategies and services to increase sales as a vital component of fast growth. Three successful entrepreneurs share their stories on how their super-sized sales accelerated the rapid growth of their companies.

Shazi Visram
Founder and CEO
Happy Family

Shari Spiro
CEO
Ad Magic Games

Cindy Monroe
Founder and CEO
Thirty-One Gifts

HAPPY FAMILY

SHAZI VISRAM,
FOUNDER
AND CEO

City, State:
New York, NY

Year Founded:
2003

Year Won 50 Fastest:
2013

Gross Revenues:

2008:	$ 1,856,356
2010:	$ 13,306,319
2012:	$ 62,761,000

Business overview:
Happy Family offers a complete line of organic meals
and snacks for babies and toddlers, as well as snacks for
older kids and adults.

To what do you attribute your success:
"Happy Family has a very big vision to change the way
children are fed in our country, which corresponds to a
significant market need. However, our success is attributed to the fact that we have coupled that need with a
very dedicated and experienced team to execute against
that vision."

BUILDING A BRAND
WITH SOCIAL IMPACT
AND ABUNDANCE

As the daughter of immigrants, Shazi Visram saw at a
young age what was possible through hard work when
you have passion and a vision. "My dream was to start

a business that could create social impact, as well as abundance. The best way I saw to make an impact was to create a brand that encouraged parents to start thinking about their children's health when they were babies, then focus on sustainable organic choices to help children's bodies grow up healthy, happy, and strong."

Twelve years ago, there were not many organic baby-food options on the market—let alone premium offerings. Happy Family sought to democratize organic baby-food options for everyday customers with an accessible price point.

A MISSION-BASED BUSINESS

Visram believes that part of her success is having a dedicated team that deeply believes in the mission with the talent to execute against it. She launched the brand in 2006 on Mother's Day, and 2016 marks the company's tenth anniversary.

Happy Family focuses on bringing innovations to the market that Visram describes as enlightened so that parents are truly excited about feeding their children.

Before 2009, baby food was sold in little glass jars. Spoon-feeding typically generates a lot of mess. The vision was to create a premium alternative to the jar. "We saw this new technology and recognized it would be an amazing format for baby food. It is a foil and plastic-lined pouch with a spout and cap that allows for a really high-quality, convenient product with no mess involved."

The food can be squeezed directly onto a spoon. "As the child grows into a toddler, you can hide a lot of veg-

etables in the pouch, so that they don't recognize they are eating them. It's a great way to sneak them in."

Introducing a nonglass container in 2009 turned around the baby food business. It was also environmentally friendly: the pouch has only 10 percent of the carbon footprint of a glass jar. Happy Family was able to ride a huge wave of commercial success. "It changed the game in baby food. If you walk down the grocery aisle today, all you see is pouches. A number of brands followed suit."

Visram is proud to say that Happy Family was the very first baby food sold in a pouch at Target. "When we watched moms at Target walk past our product on the shelves, stop and pick them up, and then fill their carts, I knew we had something."

That was the tipping point for Happy Family. The company earned $6 million in 2009 and more than doubled it—to $13 million—the following year.

SPENT THE MAJORITY OF HER TIME RAISING MONEY

Having earned an MBA from Columbia, Visram describes the beginning days of her startup as "a little fast and loose." It took two years to develop the necessary discipline and rigor involved in using financial tools. "In the beginning, we were taking so many chances and making so many investments in innovation. We were not supersophisticated in how we vetted them financially."

To her surprise, the majority of her time as an entrepreneur was spent raising money to fund the business. "I never really knew how hard it would be to raise the kind of money we needed to keep the business afloat and growing. That was a bit of a shock. I would have expected it to last us twice as long as it did. Through

the years, I learned to raise more money, and also more often. I did not think it would take $23 million of equity to get our business to where it is today. It was a great learning experience."

LEARN TO FAIL
FAST

Happy Family has a good track record for launching a product and recognizing whether it will be a hit, then creating metrics around whether or not to keep it in the line.

Although she said she did not take on a challenge thinking she was going to fail, Visram learned to recognize quickly when a mistake was made. "We have learned to fail fast. We launched products that would go to market, and the acceptance just wasn't there. But I had such a deep and emotional attachment to the product I had trouble letting go." The company has become more methodical about its innovation pipeline.

Recognizing that a mom's needs are constantly changing, the company now approaches marketing new products more cautiously, with a better understanding of trial and error. "We are trying hard to meet consumer needs and give them something they are excited about. Sometimes you hit the nail on the head and sometimes not. Most times, not."

SURROUND
YOURSELF WITH
SUPPORTIVE AND
POSITIVE PEOPLE

Visram believes it is helpful to learn from people who have done what you are doing and who have made the same mistakes. Having a strong mentor or group of mentors/advisors who can eventually become an advisory board to turn to for advice and guidance is critical at each stage of growth.

Being willing to change and adapt is a strong attribute for an early-stage entrepreneur that can mean the difference between success and failure. Visram urges entrepreneurs to have a strong business plan, understand the market, and be open to criticism/feedback.

She also stresses the need to surround yourself with truly supportive and positive people. "There is so much negativity associated with being an early-stage entrepreneur. There are so many pitfalls, and ups and downs, and tough moments when you have to make tough choices. Be around people who believe in you and can see your passion and vision. They give you better advice and better emotional support, and that increases your confidence and allows you to be a better leader."

FIND WAYS TO FEEL SUPPORTED

In the early days of her business, Visram spent time at her alma mater, Columbia Business School, working with the entrepreneurship department. She took full advantage of the networking resources available to her. Finding a community of like-minded entrepreneurs and being named the number-one ranked company in the 2013 Women Presidents' Organization 50 Fastest-Growing Women-Owned/Led Companies was also a good source of support.

In addition, Visram attracted the attention of some major business advocates. "American Express has been pivotal for us. We were featured in a couple of campaigns that really put our business on the map. They have always offered such strong resources for small businesses. As we've grown, we've taken lots of advantage."

Happy Family is certified as a B Corp, a type of company that uses the power of business to solve social and environmental problems, is purpose driven, and creates benefits for all stakeholders, not just shareholders. Being certified provides a business a platform for socially responsible accountability to measure the impact a business makes on the world. They helped create metrics in terms of how Happy Family should be run, from employment issues to environmental guidelines, with regard to how to source packaging and raw goods.

The focus on sales is constant, as Happy Family is built on a national sales model that supports new moms coming into the category every year. Working with retailers in grocery, mass merchandisers, and specialty and natural food stores, as well as online, requires optimizing relationship management. Visram is now selling in thirty-two other markets.

"We are constantly telling the story of our products and why they are so great but also how we make them and why we make them. And that's a really huge piece of our business."

Visram considers herself an adept salesperson. Whenever she believes in something, she becomes passionate. "When you have a product you believe in and you are explaining it to a potential customer, you are giving them a gift. You are doing them a favor because they will benefit from knowing about it."

Raising money is also a sales process. "You are selling your vision, your company. You are selling your equity in your business, your dream, passion, and story. You are basically selling projections of what you are going to do in the future. That requires a lot of confidence."

Visram says selling a product is easy. "It's literally the same thing as bragging about your child."

In her heart, Visram believes that there is no better salesperson for her company than she. But she can't do it all and relies on a strong sales team. "You have to find the right skills, analytics, and ability to slice and dice the data and tell a really compelling story. But it is really important to make sure whoever is selling your product is a believer."

Constant training on new products is an ongoing learning experience to make sure everyone is aligned with, focused on, and tracking against strong metrics to meet sales goals.

OPPORTUNITIES AND CHALLENGES

Visram cautions small and mid-sized businesses that are tempted by retailers offering very big deals. "The challenge is to stick to your guns and make sure you make the best decision for your business. That can be very hard because the potential for big sales is so tempting. But making the wrong choices can damage your business and your brand."

The challenge for Happy Family is to find strong distributors and partners aligned with its mission and vision. The strategy is to continue to grow and increase distribution at shelf, provide constant innovation and excellent service to customers and retailers, and remain relevant in a way that reflects the company's vision.

"Make sure you have a great product that people want and that you can sell it and make a strong margin. Then invest in credible salespeople. That's a no-brainer: one, two, and three."

- Have a strong mentor or group of mentors/advisors who can eventually become your board of directors to turn to for advice and guidance at each stage of growth.

- Be pragmatic and smart. Have a strong business plan and understand your market.

- Develop adaptability as an attribute, and be open to criticism/ feedback. The willingness to change and adapt is a strong attribute for an early-stage entrepreneur that can mean the difference between success and failure.

- Learn to fail fast.

- Find a community of like-minded entrepreneurs for support.

- Do business with strong distributors and partners who are aligned with your mission and vision. Don't be tempted by big deals that might be the wrong decision.

- Develop the necessary discipline and rigor around using financial tools.

- Raise more money than you think you will need to keep the business afloat and growing.

- Make sure whoever is selling your product is a believer. Find the right skills, analytics, and ability to slice and dice the data and tell a really compelling story.

AD MAGIC GAMES

SHARI SHAPIRO,
PRESIDENT
AND FOUNDER

City, State:
Netcong, NJ

Year Founded:
1998

Year Won 50 Fastest:
2015

Gross Revenues:
Grew 300 percent from 2010 to 2014

Business overview:
Ad Magic Games is one of the fastest-growing and most successful, independent, custom-tabletop game printers in the US.

To what do you attribute your success:
"Being experienced enough at the time a big opportunity presented itself."

SHE STARTED BY PRINTING MONEY

Shari Spiro started out in the printing industry, working in a company owned by her then-father-in-law. That was when she fell in love with manufacturing sheet-fed vinyl.

After all she was, technically, printing money.

The company was one of the first to use holographic foil and manufactured credit cards for major credit card issuers. They also made the ubiquitous promotional

wallet cards with inspirational greetings. And they made millions of them.

When the company went out of business, Spiro was designated to finish all the work in process. Essentially, it meant starting a new company.

One day a deck of cards the company had manufactured came across her desk. Making playing cards was easy: they were always the same size and shape. She thought it would be a prudent business venture to make more. So she built a website. Her custom playing cards quickly became the number-one website on Google.

A prospective client called who was in the midst of a Kickstarter campaign for a game called Cards Against Humanity. The games began shipping in 2011. What started out as a tiny project became a worldwide phenomenon. "It was like having a hit song," Spiro said. Making this game also taught her a valuable lesson: you never know who is going to become your biggest client.

She had an "aha" moment when she went to her first game industry trade show. It proved to be an environment in which she felt right at home. "I fit right in with the nerds playing games and realized it was where I belonged."

COMPANY CULTURE DETERMINES HOW PEOPLE ARE TREATED

Before she started Ad Magic, working at other jobs had left her frustrated. She said she was listened to only once after she repeatedly begged for a fax machine. And even that took two months.

Applying what she had learned not to do from those experiences helped create Spiro's current reality. "When I started running my own company, I knew I had to listen to people and treat them with respect. They have valid things to say. They are in the day-to-day grind and know what's going on." When someone comes to her with a problem, Spiro listens to what they have to say. That way she can fix it.

IT'S ALL ABOUT THE TEAM

Spiro believes she is only one small cog in the giant wheel of her company's rapid growth. What is most important to her is her relationship with the team and maintaining the culture of the company.

She treats people the way she would like to be treated. Passion and enthusiasm flow from the company leader. "A true team will support the team leader no matter what. You want a team that's happy and loves being led by you. I want my people to have passion. But you can't pay them to have passion."

Having printed the wildly popular card game Exploding Kittens, the most backed game in Kickstarter history, Spiro learned another valuable lesson: that she was more than a printer; she was now a valued advisor and an extension of her clients' teams.

Today her company is vertically integrated. It provides prototypes to game designers, production for those with funded games, and publishing when games are mass produced and need worldwide distribution.

She credits professional resources, such as membership in the Women Presidents' Organization, with

providing a much-needed support system. "All of a sudden, women came out of the woodwork to be supportive to me. It was an amazing experience. I met great friends, women who are running companies ten times my size and who related to what I was going through. There is nothing like talking to someone in a similar situation."

According to an April 2015 Middle Market Power Index report from American Express and Dun & Bradstreet titled "Catalyzing US Economic Growth," while smaller commercially active firms employ the largest share of the country's workforce (42 percent, compared to 28 percent in middle-market firms and 30 percent in the largest enterprises), the greatest increase in hiring has come from middle-market firms. Since 2008, private-sector employment among all commercially active businesses is up just 1.3 percent. However, among middle-market firms, employment has grown by 4.4 percent over the past six years, compared to a significantly lower 1.6 percent increase among larger enterprises and a 0.9 percent decline among smaller businesses. Put another way, fully 92 percent of the nearly 2.3 million net new jobs added by commercially active firms since 2008 have come from middle-market enterprises.

Spiro has always looked at herself as more of an educator than a salesperson. As such, she provides the requisite information and lets people draw their own

WOMEN PRESIDENTS' ORGANIZATION. Reaching Farther. Together.
WPO 50 Fastest Growing Women-Owned/Led Companies Guide to Growth Sponsored by American Express

138

conclusions. "In my business, you can't 'sell' anyone something. You are either quoting what they already need or educating them about what they think they need. Then they decide."

MORE EDUCATION THAN SALES

Spiro began delegating the sales function in the early days of being in business, when she grew past $250K. In building an effective sales team, she looks for basics. They must be able to stay calm, be willing to learn, and be dedicated. "They have to learn about printing. They have to have the ability to concentrate, to follow through, and do mathematical calculations."

She also takes them to trade shows to meet game designers and to gain empathy for what designers are going through. After having developed games over a period of years, she says, "We're printing people's dreams."

AN ONLINE SALES MODEL

Spiro built the business through online search optimization through organic placement and later used Web-based key-word advertising to drive sales. As her business grew, Spiro stopped advertising on the Web and relied on word of mouth. She is now in the enviable position of not needing to advertise.

When she started her company, Spiro was selling to a mature market. Now the focus has shifted to a growth market, owing to the potential with crowdfunding. "We pride ourselves as being the place for the 'life after Kickstarter.' I predicted that this new market was going to have incredible growth. And it did. I was right."

Now manufacturing mostly card and board games, as well as a few electronic ones, Spiro has moved into mass market and adapted different sales models, networking with designers and professional inventors. Clients now put her company's name on their products. She and her team attend trade shows all over the world.

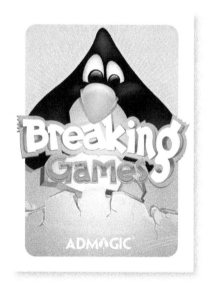

Products compete in multiple market sectors, pursuing different customers in constantly changing channels. "We take on anything. We love the idea of manufacturing something that hasn't been done before."

One of the most challenging projects that had never been done before was putting a thirty-card foil pack inside an ice pop. It required working with China; making

a model; retrofitting a cutting machine; and bringing in special sealers, food-safe dye, and foil packs. Once manufactured, they had to be shipped cross-country in fifty-five hours on a tight deadline in a freezer truck to a trade show in Seattle on Labor Day weekend. "Once they got to the sidewalk in the ice cream truck, I spent the entire trade show watching people eating ice pops. I could not believe we did it."

Exporting is a challenge. Spiro says the wins do not always outweigh the challenges, so consider all resources available to help expand your business offshore. American Express's Grow Global program is an available exporting resource to help get middle-market companies on the path to expanding business internationally and boosting profits.

TIPS FROM
SHARI SHAPIRO

- Become a valued advisor to your clients, not just a supplier.

- Make sure no client is ever unhappy. If something is wrong, fix it.

- To keep clients happy, deliver the perfect product. This is the best sales strategy.

- Learn about freight if you are considering export. While the wins do not always outweigh the challenges, the more you can learn about shipping, international freight, import/export practices, and tax systems of major markets throughout the world, the safer your export experiences will be.

- Be sure you can cover costs if something goes wrong. Try to maintain a comfortable margin; selling at a discount or too close to cost can be dangerous.

- Do what you say. Make sure you can actually deliver on a promise.

- Treat everyone with the same respect. A very small order may turn into the biggest one you ever had.

THIRTY-ONE GIFTS

thirty-one

**CINDY MONROE,
FOUNDER
AND CEO**

City, State:
Columbus, OH

Year Founded:
2003

Year Won 50 Fastest:
2014

Gross revenues:

2009:	$ 38,013,332
2011:	$ 482,246,758
2013:	$ 760,178,567

Business overview:
Thirty-One Gifts, LLC is a direct seller of exclusive, stylish, and functional purses, totes, fashion accessories, and organizing solutions.

To what do you attribute your success:
"Being purposeful, curious, hardworking, and flexible would be the traits that have helped me be a successful entrepreneur in a fast-growing business. I have also had to chase after knowledge and wisdom to become the leader I strive to be. Surrounding myself with mentors and wise leaders in and out of our company has also played a significant role in our success."

**NOT YOUR MOTHER'S
TUPPERWARE**

Cindy Monroe was young, newly married, and in college when she started working in direct sales to help pay

the family bills. She started Thirty-One Gifts in her basement when she was twenty-eight years old. The direct-sales company offers a diverse mix of "giftable" items—fashion accessories, home-organization products, totes, and lunch boxes—and personalizes products by embroidering initials and names. Consultants sell through what have been traditionally known as "home parties."

The name "Thirty-One Gifts" comes from Proverbs 31, the twentieth book of the Old Testament, which describes the attributes and the importance of a "virtuous woman." It speaks to being a woman of integrity while finding balance as a wife, mother, business owner, and support to the community.

"We are a family of individuals who share a passion for empowering women and who are committed to celebrate, encourage, and reward others for who they are."

The mission of Thirty-One Gifts is to give women the earning potential and flexibility of running their own businesses, providing them with all the tools and support necessary to find success and build a new career. Connecting with an extensive network helps build meaningful relationships and offers empowerment.

"I wanted to provide the opportunity for other women to be able to dream big, have their own business, and a little extra income."

IT'S ABOUT GETTING TO THE "WHY"

Monroe understands the appeal of the "why"—the power of earning a little additional cash to cover unanticipated expenses and some of life's extras, such as vacations, education, and debt.

Getting to their own "why" has been a critical component of motivating sales consultants. Monroe wants to know exactly what their definition of success looks like and how freedom from debt makes them feel.

A DECADE OF ROCKET-SHIP GROWTH

In its first ten years, Thirty-One Gifts experienced supersonic growth, from zero to $700 million. Monroe quickly crossed the midmarket range, achieving $10 million in revenue during her fifth or sixth year in business.

"We believe in the power of relationships. While the modern world says relationships can thrive from a distance, we know better. We're passionate about bringing women together and creating opportunities for them to shop face-to-face while building new friendships."

From its humble beginnings, the company has grown into one of the most successful direct-selling businesses in the world, with more than ninety thousand independent sales consultants across the US and Canada.

Total company sales

#3
Party plan company behind Mary Kay and Tupperware

#28
in 2015 DSA*Global 100

#14
in 2015 DSA North America 50

* DSA= Direct Selling Association

THAT MAKE-OR-BREAK MOMENT

Reaching the five-year mark was Monroe's first major benchmark. "I wanted to make sure my company was valid and that I could build on it when I hit that five-year mark, that I was actually profitable. That's when I realized, wow, I had made it to that mark."

IN THE NEWS **4 TIMES** EACH DAY

CIRCULATION OF **906 MILLION** ANNUALLY

She learned about pitfalls through trial and error. "Once you've been in business for five or six years and start to enter mid-market, you learn from some of your mistakes and start to foresee them."

When she was a smaller business, gut instinct and a sense of passion and mission helped Monroe make the right decisions. "But when you start growing into that midmarket and you are making million-dollar decisions, you don't want to trust your gut as much. You want black-and-white numbers and metrics to focus on."

USING MISSION AS
THE NORTH STAR

One of the most important tips Monroe shares with other women-led companies as they scale their businesses for growth is having clarity of mission and making sure every decision aligns with that mission.

"The mission of the company was very important to me, and that was something around what my vision was for the business. For me, women are the key audience. It is really around supporting them and having a business, not just selling products."

Monroe attributes her fast growth to being in the right place at the right time, with affordable products—and retail prices that average $25–$30. "We were very fresh within our industry and our products at a time when families needed extra income." After the 2008 recession, families in the Midwest were particularly hard hit. Thirty-One Gifts offered an appealing opportunity to augment their income.

Middle-market firms appear to have borne the brunt of the impact of the 2007–2009 recession on business revenues. According to an April 2015 Middle Market Power Index report from American Express and Dun & Bradstreet titled "Catalyzing US Economic Growth," in a year-over-year analysis of

revenue growth over the past six years, middle-market firm revenues declined nearly 30 percent between 2008 and 2009, recovered well by 2011, and have seen modest growth since then. Changes in year-over-year revenues have been much less variable among firms with less than $10 million in revenues and firms with $1 billion or more in revenues.

A pivotal moment was making the decision to move her business from Tennessee to Ohio, leaving family and some employees behind. "I came to that decision because the business was growing, and we were having a hard time finding executives who lived in town." She was already working with a sourcing partner in Ohio and traveling there once a month. "I chose to invest in the people of the business. And the talent and people I was finding were in Ohio."

After the move, the business exploded, experiencing a whopping 1,900 percent growth in a four-year time period.

MAKING VALUABLE CONNECTIONS WITH OTHER WOMEN ENTREPRENEURS

When Monroe looks back on the early days, she wishes she had joined professional membership organizations sooner than she did to connect with role models who shared the same values.

"I really wish someone had tapped me on the shoulder and said, 'You really need to do this.' I think I could have grown professionally and would have made some different decisions if I had the support."

After moving to Ohio, she joined the local chapter of the Women Presidents' Organization, then its Zenith group. She was also part of The EY Entrepreneur of the Year® Program in Kentucky/southern Ohio.

"They say it can get lonely at the top. If you've been in the shoes of being an owner and entrepreneur, it is true. Having a 'phone a friend' is very important."

A CONSTANT NEED TO SELL

Thirty-One Gifts is built on a direct-sales model. Part of the sales appeal is the prospect of becoming a "micro entrepreneur" and the opportunity to earn extra income. It's a company built on relationships, not on e-commerce transactions. "We sell through our consultants, so we have to build upon and strengthen those relationships so they stay engaged and want to continue to represent the brand."

The ability to connect the head and the heart is what Monroe believes makes an effective salesperson. "Anytime you find a salesperson who can speak from the heart, is good at storytelling, sees the vision clearly, and wants to impact and influence someone's life with what they have to offer, that is what makes a good salesperson."

An Internet site offers training for new consultants. During a 120-day start-up period, they work with a team leader who provides one-on-one coaching. Promotion to leader happens when four to six strong sales consultants are recruited to the team. Leaders then become eligible to be sales directors who can have up to twenty to forty people on the team. They can then progress to

senior leaders, finding other women who want to start and lead their own successful sales organizations.

Using a direct-sales model with a grassroots approach, along with the ability to manufacture and house fulfillment in one city, Thirty-One Gifts is a scalable model. The company does 80 percent of its sales in twenty-five states and recently expanded into Canada.

"Canada was a very easy market for us to go into. People in the region love our product, and there is a demand for direct selling there. Some of the challenges have included the logistics of shipping from the US into Canada, website regulations, and laws governing marketing.

One of the biggest sales challenges for Thirty-One Gifts has been trying to balance promotional strategies that deliver short-term productivity with sales strategies that gain long-term growth. The question is whether to go for the short-term wins or a slow and steady productivity margin to make sure the business has a strong foundation.

TIPS FROM
CINDY MONROE

- Appoint a dedicated financial professional. Make sure the company has the requisite amount of cash and profitability that can support growth.

- Trust your gut at the beginning because passion and mission are what drive your business. When you arrive at the point of making million-dollar decisions, use metrics to forecast and foresee pitfalls.

- Make sure the mission of the company isn't just about you but around your overall vision for the business.

- Be purposeful about your business plan and the actions to carry it out.

- Feel confident in how you are leading the business.

- Keep your eye on the competition, but keep distractions from what other companies are doing to a minimum.

- Have a strong compensation plan with effective incentives.

- Know your customers and test new products: measure what they are purchasing and where to make strategic decisions about expanding into new markets.

- Use discounting strategies to drive sales volume for a limited time. Squeezing profit margins can help accommodate promotional periods.

Printed in the USA
CPSIA information can be obtained
at www.ICGtesting.com
JSHW072028140824
68134JS00044B/3831